Ach **QTS**

...ork

Behaviour
for **Learning**
in the Primary School

Achieving QTS

meeting the **professional standards framework**

Behaviour for **Learning**

in the Primary School

Kate Adams

LearningMatters

First published in 2009 by Learning Matters Ltd.

British Library Cataloguing in Publication Data
A CIP record for this book is available from the British Library.

ISBN: 978 1 84445 188 3

Cover design by Topics – The Creative Partnership
Text design by Code 5 Design Associates Ltd.
Project management by Deer Park Productions, Tavistock
Typeset by PDQ Typesetting Ltd, Newcastle under Lyme
Printed and bound in Great Britain by Bell & Bain Ltd, Glasgow

Learning Matters
33 Southernhay East
Exeter EX1 1NX
Tel: 01392 215560
info@learningmatters.co.uk
www.learningmatters.co.uk

Contents

1
Behaviour: why you need to care

Chapter objectives

By the end of this chapter you should be able to:

- **describe the types of behaviour you might encounter in primary schools;**
- **understand that behaviour and learning are linked;**
- **know the three key components of the Behaviour 4 Learning approach;**
- **understand that the concept of Behaviour 4 Learning applies to you as well as to children.**

This chapter addresses the following Professional Standards for QTS:

Q2, Q10, Q30, Q31

Links to: Every Child Matters (ECM); Primary National Strategy; spiritual, moral, social and cultural development (SMSC); personal, social and health and citizenship education (PSHCE); special educational needs (SEN); inclusive education.

Introduction

Excitement and anticipation are prevalent when details of placements are publicised. Crowds of students hover around the noticeboard and typical comments overheard include: 'Oh that is such a lovely, friendly school, you are so lucky', 'I can't go there, the children are so badly behaved, I'll never control them' and 'That's a fantastic school, the children all work really hard and get great results'.

Many factors will affect your response to the school you have been placed in – how far you'll have to travel, whether the school has a good reputation or not, if you know anyone who works there or has had a placement there. You will inevitably be concerned about the school's standing, whether it be based on information gleaned from the 'grapevine' and/or through research into their Ofsted reports and place in league tables. One of the key factors underlying your reaction is likely to be the school's reputation for children's behaviour. If the school has a large number of children with challenging behaviour, you may be apprehensive about how this will affect your performance in the classroom.

Your concern about children's behaviour is shared by many other trainees and newly qualified teachers (NQTs) alike. The Association of Teachers and Lecturers (ATL) surveyed students and NQTs and discovered that 94 per cent of student teachers and 97 per cent of NQTs identified pupil discipline as the most important issue for them (ATL, 2006). This is understandable – after all, if children are misbehaving, you cannot teach effectively and they won't learn.

Hopefully you will feel prepared to face the challenge of the children's potential misbehaviour before you arrive at school. However, Ofsted's report *Managing challenging behaviour* (2005a) states that NQTs often report that their initial training contained little specific guidance on understanding and managing children's behaviour. Ofsted (2005a) acknowledges that training in this area requires more than one or two sessions and should be part of a longer-term strategy which continues to support you over the course of your career. Fortunately, the Training and Development Agency for Schools' (TDA) annual survey of NQTs shows that the teaching of behaviour management in initial teacher training (ITT) is improving. Their report of those who successfully completed their initial teacher training in England in 2005/2006 shows an increase in the number who rated their training for this area positively. During that period, 71 per cent of the 11,000 respondents rated this aspect of their training as good or very good – compared with 59 per cent in 2003 (TDA, 2007a). While this provision still has considerable room for improvement, this is encouraging news.

Behaviour: why you need to care

Children's positive behaviour is important for a range of reasons. Firstly, and possibly of most immediate concern to you, is that in order to achieve qualified teacher status (QTS), you will be required to meet a set of standards laid out by the TDA (2007b). Three of these include explicit reference to children's behaviour. Trainees are required to:

- *Demonstrate the positive values, attitudes and behaviour they expect from children and young people (Q2)*
- *Have a knowledge and understanding of a range of teaching, learning and behaviour management strategies and know how to use and adapt them . . . (Q10)*
- *Establish a clear framework for classroom discipline to manage learners' behaviour constructively and promote their self-control and independence (Q31)*

The QTS standards are underpinned by five key outcomes identified in the government's *Every Child Matters: change for children* (ECM) policy (DfES, 2004), which were subsequently laid out in the Children Act 2004. ECM arose following the death of Victoria Climbié in 2000. Victoria was an eight-year-old girl who lived with her great aunt and her aunt's partner in London. Her aunt and partner tortured her, and despite previous involvement of social workers, doctors and police, the horrific abuse led to Victoria's death. ECM built on existing plans to strengthen preventative services to protect children (DCSF, undated). ECM has five key outcomes for all children, which are:

- *Be healthy*
- *Stay safe*
- *Enjoy and achieve*
- *Make a positive contribution*
- *Achieve economic well-being*

(DfES, 2004, page 10)

Anti-social behaviour beyond the school gates

In the Every Child Matters agenda, behaviour is a focus in the two outcomes 'stay safe' and 'make a positive contribution'. It aims to keep children *safe from anti-social behaviour in and out of school*, and help them *engage in law-abiding and positive behaviour in and out of school*. It also aims to prevent them from engaging in bullying behaviour (DfES, 2004, page 10). These outcomes draw attention to further key reasons for caring about behaviour – issues of safety both within and outside the school, self-respect and respect for others.

The emphasis on behaviour beyond the school gates is a sound reminder that your role as a teacher carries positive influence on children out of school hours. Further, their behaviour outside of school can also be reflected in the classroom. Part of many trainees' apprehension about managing children's behaviour will have stemmed from the media. For example, high-profile cases such as the fatal stabbing of 10-year-old schoolboy Damilola Taylor on his way home from school in 2000 show the tragic consequences of extreme anti-social behaviour among teenagers. Following Damilola's tragic death, Southwark council in south London began a scheme in which some schools had police officers on their premises. By 2003, police officers were on the premises of 100 schools in London, Manchester and Birmingham (Hackett, 2003).

We need to care about behaviour because children and young adults need to be safe, and feel safe, on the streets as well as in school. That right to be safe, of course, also extends to you and legislation is in place to support that right. For example, the Crime and Disorder Act 1998 introduced Anti-Social Behaviour Orders (ASBOs) which ban recipients from acting in a public place in the manner which gave rise to the Order. Schools can be named as a public place in an ASBO. Fortunately it is only the minority of young people who will be given ASBOs or be the perpetrators of violent behaviour. It is important to acknowledge that behaviour is not simply an issue for trainees and teachers – it is also a concern for children, young people and their parents (DCSF, 2007), as well as for all other members of the community. Inevitably, then, behaviour is also an issue for teacher trainers and policy-makers (EPPI, 2004). In short, every-one in society is a stakeholder in the behaviour of young people.

In essence the education system has a significant role to play in nurturing children to become responsible citizens who can make informed choices in their lives. The non-statu-tory guidelines for personal, social, health and citizenship education (PSHCE) are followed by many primary schools, which helps give children the knowledge and skills they need to make healthy choices, manage their feelings and deal with moral and social issues that arise. Alongside PSHCE is the statutory requirement for the spiritual, moral, social and cultural (SMSC) development of children, which underpins the National Curriculum. Together, PSHCE and SMSC can contribute to helping children act responsibly and morally, in turn creating a safe environment.

Let's return to the classroom and take a closer look at your role in it, the types of behaviour you may encounter, and explore another crucial reason for caring about behaviour: the link between behaviour and learning.

Behaviour and learning

It may be tempting to think that the management of behaviour is an 'add-on' to your teach-ing, but this would be a mistake. In fact, another key reason for ensuring positive behaviour in school is its link with learning. Behaviour and learning are inextricably linked, as will become clear throughout this book.

The link between behaviour and learning has long been recognised. In 1989 a committee of enquiry was set up to explore behaviour in schools, which resulted in the Elton Report, entitled *Discipline in schools* (1989). This report still has much relevance today. It stated that children can learn well only if they have a purposeful and peaceful classroom environment in which to work. Similarly, in 2002, the government appointed a panel of experts to again enquire into discipline in schools, resulting in the Steer Report – a series of four published from 2005 to 2008. The first, entitled *Learning behaviour,* (2005, page 2) subscribes to the view that *the quality of learning, teaching and behaviour in schools are inseparable issues*. Government policy also emphasises this link – the Primary National Strategy, launched in 2003 through the document *Excellence and enjoyment – a strategy for primary schools* (DfES, 2003a, page 4), aims to focus on raising standards, but combines this with *making learning fun*. If teachers can enable children to enjoy their learning, it is increasingly likely that their behaviour will be positive.

Similarly, Ofsted (2005a, page 15) endorses this link, commenting that in their own inspections, *effective teaching and learning is a key to encouraging good behaviour and engaging with those pupils who have the most difficult behaviour*. Ofsted recognise that the poor behaviour of some children affects not only their learning but also the learning of others.

The government actively seeks to improve children's attendance, behaviour and learning through its policies. For example, they spent £470 million on the Behaviour and Attendance Strategy, and their Improving Behaviour in Schools Programme recognises that staff, parents and pupils all have a role to play in ensuring positive learning environments for all who attend school.

REFLECTIVE TASK

Consider the range of behaviours you have observed in the classroom. What kinds of positive behaviours have you seen that supported children's learning? What kinds of behaviours have you seen which inhibited learning? How did one child's disruptive behaviour affect others' learning?

Behaviour, learning and special educational needs

For some children, particularly those with special educational needs (SEN), difficulties in learning can lead to frustration which manifests in poor behaviour, while children with social, emotional and behavioural difficulties (SEBD) can exhibit behaviour which prevents their own learning as well as that of their classmates. The government's policy on inclusion has increased the number of children with such difficulties in mainstream schools (Garner, 2005). Westwood (2006) states that broadly, inclusion refers to the right of every child, irrespective of gender, ethnicity, social class, ability or disability, to be educated within a mainstream classroom. There are, however, differing conceptions of inclusion (Farrell and Ainscow, 2002) and you are directed to the literature on this topic for a more in-depth consideration of the history and theoretical underpinning of this important area.

For members of school communities, the impact of inclusive education has been significant. Many have welcomed the drive to educate all children together (irrespective of whether or not they have special educational needs) because it works towards social justice. However, others have raised concerns that mainstream classrooms are not the most effective place for educating children with severe SEN (Westwood, 2006). In extreme cases, violence is a major concern for staff and pupils alike, albeit as Ofsted (2005a) state, they are rare and carried out by a very small proportion of pupils. Chapter 6 explores SEN and SEBD in more detail.

Managing behaviour

Throughout the course of your training you will become extremely familiar with the term 'managing behaviour'. It is the theme of countless books written to support trainees and NQTs, an essential section in every book on how to be an effective teacher, and of course as you have already seen, a term used in the QTS standards. But what does the term actually mean?

CASE STUDY

What does 'managing behaviour' mean?

Emma was a reasonably confident trainee who was about to embark on her final placement. In her previous placements she had successfully engaged children in learning but was nervous about her final one because of the reputation of the bad behaviour exhibited by a group of children in her Year 6 class. As she talked through her anxieties with her tutor, it appeared that she had taken the term 'managing behaviour' to mean that she had to gain control over children who were not behaving.

Emma is not alone in her misunderstanding. The EPPI-Centre report (2004) noted concern that too often teachers perceive behaviour management to mean establishing control over disruptive pupils. If you share this view, such a perception can place significant but unnecessary stress upon you while you are training, partly because you cannot anticipate and prepare for all pupil responses that you may experience in school. The term 'managing behaviour' involves different components and is more wide-reaching than simply stopping bad behaviour.

A large component, detailed in the next chapter, relates to the provision of practical techniques for the prevention of challenging behaviour, rewarding positive behaviour, giving sanctions for negative behaviour and implementing strategies to deal with different types of misbehaviour. No trainee can survive without such strategies and knowledge, and all trainees and experienced teachers alike use them on a daily basis. However, the word 'management' also relates to your provision of a strong ethos of mutual respect which also supports learning. It is important for you to know that, throughout your career, you will have a wide range of support to help you achieve positive behaviour in the classroom. This support is an important aspect of government policy which recognises that *behaviour is a critical issue* and helps schools in teaching positive behaviour through the Primary National Strategy (DfES, 2003a, page 8). The full range of support will be identified throughout this book, and explored in detail in Chapter 8.

Managing behaviour, therefore, consists of different components and is not simply about controlling disruptive children. Prior to exploring those components in depth in the following chapters, we will first consider the forms that disruptive behaviour is likely to take.

The nature of disruptive behaviours in the classroom

While it is natural for you to be anxious about your ability to support children in their learning, including achieving positive behaviour to enhance that learning, official documents are keen to reassure you that overall, highly challenging behaviour is found only in a minority of primary schools. Ofsted (2005b, page 3) judged that behaviour was at least satisfactory or better in 90 per cent of primary schools in 2003/2004. In their report for 2006/2007, Ofsted (2007) combined their primary and secondary judgements to declare that behaviour is good or outstanding in 88 per cent of all maintained schools. They observed that only 8 per cent of primary schools had behaviour which was 'just satisfactory', compared with 29 per cent of secondary schools.

The Steer Report (2005) supports the view that the majority of pupils work hard and behave well. It acknowledges that there are exceptions where serious misbehaviour, including violence, occurs, but emphasises that these are rare and often take place in schools which have major failings in other areas, as defined by Ofsted. Similarly, Ofsted (2007) observes that behaviour is rarely inadequate across a school as a whole. More recently, the third part of the Steer Report (Steer, 2008) emphasises that the number of schools with serious behaviour problems is at the lowest level ever recorded. So, what kinds of behaviours are you likely to encounter in schools?

Low-level disruption

The Elton Report (1989) noted that the most frequent forms of misbehaviour were low-level disruption. Interestingly, this situation has not changed over the years, as more recent reports have similar findings. Ofsted (2005a,b) note that low-level disruption is still the most commonly reported type of misbehaviour in schools. The term refers to behaviours which are generally inoffensive, do not hurt others, but can be frustrating and distracting. These include talking while the teacher is talking, leaving one's seat, calling out or not having equipment (Rogers, 1998). Others frequently encountered are tapping an object on a table, leaning back on a chair, giggling instead of concentrating and making silly comments at inappropriate times (Hayes, 2003). For the teacher, such behaviours can be frustrating. Significantly, these minor behaviours can also disrupt other children's learning.

Garner (2005) and Rogers (1998) point out that defining inappropriate behaviour or rating it as 'low' or 'high' is not necessarily straightforward because of the subjective elements. One teacher may be able to ignore a child's tapping of a pen against the table, while another teacher may find it extremely annoying. Further, a teacher's level of frustration can also be affected by other factors such as their mood or the time of day, so on Monday morning they might be tolerant of pen tapping but by the end of term, at the end of a day of indoor playtimes, their patience might be considerably lower.

CASE STUDY
The frustration of low-level behaviour
Tom, a trainee, was undertaking observations in a Year 4 class on the types of low-level disruptive behaviour that occurred over a week. He indicated surprise at the number he noted. In order of frequency they were: calling out, looking for a pencil, asking to go to the toilet, deliberately making noises, playfully hiding other children's possessions, distracting other children and answering back. Tom commented that while none of these caused distress to other children, nor seriously impeded the progress of a lesson, they were a constant source of frustration to the teacher and the TA. *There are days*, the teacher told him, *when I feel exasperated. All I want to do is teach but I seem to spend so much time dealing with minor interruptions*.

High-level disruption

While the majority of misbehaviour in primary schools is low-level, there are cases of high-level disruption in some schools. Visser (2000), Rooney (2002) and Westwood (2006) state that children with emotional and behavioural difficulties (EBD) present a significant challenge to schools becoming inclusive settings. As Rooney (2002) notes, many parents and teachers have expressed concern that children with very challenging behaviour not only disturb the learning of others but can also be a threat to the safety of others.

> **REFLECTIVE TASK**
>
> Have you encountered violent children in any of your placements? What form did their behaviour take? Why do you think they behaved in this way?

A major area of concern for children, teachers and parents alike is bullying, which involves a range of unacceptable behaviours, some of which are physical, but not all. Oliver and Candappa of the Thomas Coram Research Unit conducted research into children and young people's views of bullying for the charity ChildLine (DfES, 2003b). They discovered that bullying was widespread, with 51 per cent of primary school children questioned believing that it was either a 'big problem' or 'quite a problem' in their school. More Year 5 children (51%) reported being bullied that term, than did pupils in Year 8 (28%) (DfES, 2003b, page 3). However, the research showed that bullying did not occur equally in every school. Further, while schools have anti-bullying policies, the children in this study appeared to be receiving mixed messages about bullying and the authors argue that policies need to take into account children's social worlds. Policies, they suggest, should begin with pupils' experiences and should consider the consequences for children of telling someone they are being bullied.

The government acts against bullying and has launched different initiatives to help schools and their children. For example, the DfES (2000) provided a pack entitled *Don't suffer in silence* which includes a video, to support schools in establishing a whole-school policy that explores the nature of bullying, children's views, methods of detection, and how to work with victims and families. In 2003 an Anti-Bullying Charter was launched which offers practical advice for schools, and the DCSF website hosts information pages for pupils, teachers and parents (see www.dcsf.gov.uk/bullying/index.shtml).

A final growing area of anxiety in some parts of the country is the increasing number of children bringing alcohol, drugs or weapons onto school premises. While secondary schools are the main focus of these concerns, primary teachers in these localities are particularly alert to these potential threats to the safety of those in their schools. In the third part of Steer's review of behaviour (Steer, 2008), there are recommendations that the power of search for teachers be extended to include a broad range of items, not only weapons. Fortunately, for most of you working in primary schools throughout the country, instances of children bringing alcohol, drugs or weapons into school will never be an issue.

The Behaviour for Learning (B4L) approach

The misbehaviour of some children in a primary classroom is inevitable, even if it is mainly of a low-level nature. Given the importance of positive behaviour for the reasons outlined above, the TDA is active in helping you to meet the standards required. The TDA supports

ITT Professional Resource Networks (IPRNs) which are expert groups. One such IPRN is Behaviour4Learning – B4L – which helps you to foster a classroom ethos of behaviour for learning. So, what is meant by the phrase 'behaviour for learning'?

In 2004, the Evidence for Policy and Practice Information and Co-ordinating Centre (EPPI-Centre) at the Institute of Education, London, published a report which presented a systematic review of studies which explored the theoretical links to learning behaviour in school contexts which had been published between 1988 and 2002. The review had three components:

- *To examine how researchers use theories to explain learning behaviour;*
- *To explore what is known about children's learning behaviour in school contexts;*
- *To examine the utility of the review's conceptual framework for end users.*

(EPPI, 2004)

B4L conceptual framework

At the heart of the B4L approach is an emphasis on the influence of relationships upon children's learning behaviours. EPPI-Centre (2004) offers a diagram depicting their conceptual framework. See Figure 1.1.

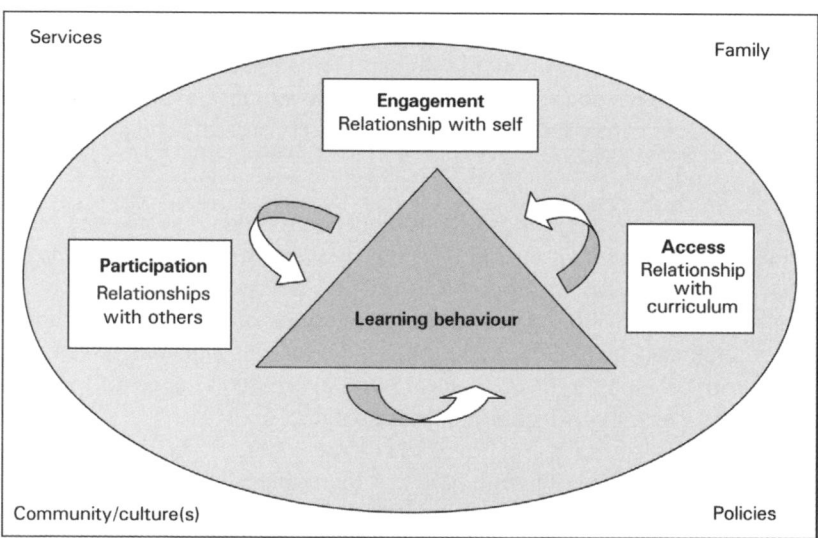

Figure 1.1. The Behaviour for Learning conceptual framework
Diagram taken from the EPPI-Centre Report (2004)

As Figure 1.1 shows, and this book explores in depth, the complexity of the variables which can affect learning behaviour is considerable. For example, relationships with self do not develop in isolation from relationships with others and relationships with curriculum. This complexity makes a definitive definition of 'learning behaviours' difficult. However, this chapter seeks to highlight the main features of a potential definition. Further, the book will take you through the different components of relationships with self, others and curriculum in separate chapters to help you gain a fuller understanding of them and how they can affect behaviour for learning.

Children's learning behaviour

The term 'learning behaviour' was described by the studies in the EPPI-Centre review (2004) in different ways, which further highlights the difficulty in offering a precise definition. However, the studies tended to suggest that behaviour which indicates learning reflects that learning in school contexts is influenced by the interaction of a range of individual, curricular and social variables.

> **REFLECTIVE TASK**
>
> Recall a lesson which you have seen or taught, where children exhibited positive behaviour for learning. What were the children doing which indicated that they were learning? What personal traits were they displaying while working?

EPP-Centre's review (2004) recorded the terms used in the studies to describe learning behaviours and found that most terms used were positive. The most common was 'engagement', found in 43 per cent of the studies. Other terms were 'collaboration', 'participation', 'communication', 'motivation', 'independent activity', 'responsiveness', 'self-regard', 'self-esteem', and 'responsibility'. For the 5–10 years age group, the most frequently observed learning behaviours were engagement, collaboration and participation. Compare these with your list compiled in the practical task above.

EPPI-Centre's review (2004) also explored the types of theories included in the studies. The researchers classified them as social (21 referents), cognitive (18 referents) and affective (17 referents). Generally, the use of these types of theories suggests that researchers were interested in the interplay of feeling, thinking and doing/interacting. However, researchers tended to link cognitive and social theories together more frequently than they linked cognitive with affective. The relevant theories are detailed in Chapters 3 to 6 in a way which also shows the usefulness of the underpinning conceptual framework in depth – showing how the interplay of different relationships can have a marked effect on shaping a child's behaviour for learning. This approach will help you to see how the theory has practical applications for you in the classroom, and will also give you guidance on how to develop your practice further.

Your behaviour for learning

Until now, the discussion about behaviour and learning has largely focused upon children. However, before you continue reading this book, pause for a moment to consider how your own approach to your placement – your behaviour – affects your learning and vice versa. As QTS Standard 2 states, you will need to *demonstrate the positive values, attitudes and behaviour [you] expect from children and young people* (TDA, 2007b, Q2).

Approach this task with as much honesty as you can. Your tutors and mentors won't need to see your answers.

PRACTICAL TASK PRACTICAL TASK **PRACTICAL TASK** PRACTICAL TASK **PRACTICAL TASK**

Read the statements below and tick the appropriate box to indicate your response to them.

		Strongly agree	Agree	Not sure	Disagree	Strongly disagree
1	I'll do everything needed to pass my placement with high grades					
2	I'll do what I need to in order to pass					
3	I want to be involved in extracurricular activities on placement					
4	I want to learn much more about specific areas of teaching					
5	I'll be happy to do whatever the teacher asks me to					
6	I will be proactive and seek tasks to assist the teacher					
7	The targets I have set myself are very challenging					
8	I'd like to help at the school fete on Sunday but I don't have the time					

Tutors, lecturers and mentors see a variety of approaches to learning in students. The vast majority of trainees are highly motivated and conscientious and this attitude is exhibited in their behaviour. Essentially, they arrive at school early with fully prepared lesson plans; if the teacher is busy they use initiative to utilise their time efficiently; they engage with children and other adults in the school to begin to build relationships with them; they stay late to prepare the classroom or take part in extracurricular activities; they seek opportunities to learn, whether it be to ask questions of staff, read policies, or find their own resources. In short, their conscientious approach is exhibited in their behaviour: they are keen to learn and display behaviours which not only reflect that desire but also facilitate learning.

If you rated questions 1 and 3–7 as 'strongly agree' or 'agree' then you are most likely to be in this category. As the descriptions for positive behaviour for learning above suggest, you probably exhibit at least some of those characteristics: you were fully engaged with tasks; collaborated with colleagues; participated in a range of activities; communicated well with children and staff; remained motivated; worked independently; were responsive to situations and suggestions and took responsibility. You are also likely to have positive self-regard and good levels of self-esteem.

Conversely, students who are unmotivated to learn convey less positive behaviours and often admit that they are undertaking training because they didn't know what else to do. It is difficult to hide a lack of commitment on an ITT course. Frequent indicators include: trainees who leave school as early as possible; do not have their file up to date; complain that their teacher has asked them to do jobs which they consider to be menial; and who claim that they are not certain of their remit because 'things were not explained properly' by the lecturers (i.e. passing the blame). Fortunately these trainees are in the minority – and cannot meet the QTS Standards. I also suspect that they are not reading this book.

For the motivated student, it is not sufficient to simply recognise the aforementioned positive qualities in yourself. In order to gain a deeper understanding of learning behaviours, you also need to examine the factors which have shaped and affected them.

REFLECTIVE TASK

What enables you to exhibit positive learning behaviour on your course? Consider the following potential factors and assess their relevance for you. Do you have high levels of motivation? Where does this motivation originate? Who or what influences your motivational levels? How do you sustain levels of motivation in times of difficulty?

Our approach to learning is affected by many things, particularly our relationships with self, with others, and with the work we are doing. While this book focuses primarily on behaviour for learning in the primary school, it will continue to ask you to reflect upon aspects of yourself. These are timely reminders that as an adult you must also be conscious of your own attitudes towards learning and how your behaviour corresponds to those attitudes – and how your approach is affected by other influences. Such insights into yourself will develop your role as a reflective practitioner, as detailed in Chapter 9. Further, your insights will deepen your understanding of children's behaviours, making you more empathic when trying to understand why a child is misbehaving.

A SUMMARY OF **KEY POINTS**

> Children's behaviour is a widespread and valid concern for most trainees.

> The majority of poor behaviour in primary schools is low-level disruption.

> Behaviour and learning are closely linked.

> The B4L approach has three major components: relationship with self, relationship with others and relationship with curriculum.

> B4L is as relevant to you as it is to the children.

MOVING *ON* > > > > > > MOVING *ON* > > > > > > MOVING *ON*

During your induction year, you will need to meet the core standards laid out by the TDA (2007b). Some of these relate specifically to behaviour management strategies, which are set out for you at the end of Chapter 2 in its 'Moving on' section. The Standards do, however, specify that your knowledge and under-standing of learning and behaviour management strategies are kept up to date (C10). For that reason it is advisable that you maintain your understanding of the behaviour for learning approach, which you can do through reading, consultation of the B4L website, and if possible through attendance at continuing profes-sional development (CPD) courses.

As a trainee you are very busy juggling study, placements and personal life. You know that you need to manage the children's behaviour effectively and because of demands on your time you need some strate-gies to help you achieve this. The following chapter provides you with a basic repertoire of strategies, but also encourages a critical approach, which will prepare you to explore the behaviour for learning approach in depth for the remainder of the book.

FURTHER READING FURTHER READING FURTHER READING FURTHER READING

Behaviour4Learning (available from www.behaviour4learning.ac.uk). In addition to covering the theoretical components of the B4L approach, the website provides a range of useful resources and links.

DCSF hosts a website on behaviour and attendance. It includes links to reports and projects and also offers guidance on a range of topics including truancy, exclusion and parenting contracts. The latest reports and strategies on behaviour are posted on the site. (The website is available at: www.dcsf.gov.uk/behaviourandattendance/index.cfm)

EPPI (2004) *A systematic review of how theories explain learning behaviour in school contexts*. The report details the key findings of the review. (You can download it from www.behaviour4learning.co.uk)

Every Child Matters: change for children (2004) London: DfES. ECM expresses the government's aim for every child and young person, from birth to age 19, to have the support they need to be healthy, stay safe, enjoy and achieve, make a positive contribution and achieve economic well-being. (Available from: www.everychildmatters.gov.uk)

Steer Report (2005) *Learning behaviour: the report of the practitioners' group on school behaviour and discipline.* This report details the findings of the enquiry and also lays out recommendations for future practice, (which are available from www.dfes.gov.uk). This is one of a series of four reports. At the time of writing, the second and third have been published (see below). By the time of this book's publication, the fourth will have been released.

REFERENCES REFERENCES REFERENCES REFERENCES REFERENCES REFERENCES

ATL (Association of Teachers and Lecturers) (2006) *Poor behaviour is an ongoing problem, ATL survey finds*. Available from www.atl.org.uk

DCSF (2007) *The Children's Plan: building brighter futures.* London: DCSF

DCSF (undated) *Background to Every Child Matters*. Available at www.everychildmatters.gov.uk/aims/background, accessed 9 June 2008

DfES (2000) *Bullying: don't suffer in silence.* London: DfES

DfES (2003a) *Excellence and enjoyment: a strategy for primary schools.* London: DfES

DfES (2003b) *Tackling bullying: listening to the views of children and young people. Summary report.* London: DfES

DfES (2004) *Every Child Matters: change for children*. London: DfES

Elton Report (1989) *Discipline in schools. Report of the committee of inquiry.* London: HMSO

EPPI (2004) *A systematic review of how theories explain learning behaviour in school contexts*. Available from: www.behaviour4learning.ac.uk, accessed 5 January 2008

Farrell, P and Ainscow, M (2002) Making special education inclusive: mapping the issues, in P Farrell, and M Ainscow (eds) *Making special education inclusive*, pp 1–12. Abingdon: David Fulton

Garner, P (2005) Behaviour for learning: a positive approach to managing classroom behaviour, in S Capel, M Leask, and T Turner (eds) *Learning to teach in the secondary school: a companion to school experience*. Abingdon: Routledge

Hackett, G (2003) Education: tackling violence in schools. *Times Online,* 9 February 2003, (available at www.timesonline.co.uk/tol/news/article869695.ece). Accessed 4 June 2008

Hayes, D (2003) *A student teacher's guide to primary school placement: learning to survive and prosper.* London: Routledge

Ofsted (2005a) *Managing challenging behaviour.* London: Ofsted. Available from: www.ofsted.gov.uk/Ofsted-home/Publications-and-research/Care/Childcare/Managing-challenging-behaviour(language)/eng-GB, accessed 20 October 2008

Ofsted (2005b) *The annual report of her majesty's chief inspector of schools 2003/2004.* London: Ofsted

Ofsted (2007) *The annual report of her majesty's chief inspector of education, children's services and skills 2006/2007.* London: The Stationery Office

Rogers, B (1998) *You know the fair rule.* Harlow: Pearson Education

Rooney, S (2002) Inclusive solutions for children with emotional and behavioural difficulties, in P Farrell and M Ainscow (eds) *Making special education inclusive,* pp 87–100. Abingdon: David Fulton

Steer, A (chair) (2008) *Behaviour review, paper 3.* Available from www.teachernet.gov.uk/docbank/index.cfm?id=12743, accessed 10 September 2008

Steer Report (2005) *Learning behaviour: The report of the practitioners' group on school behaviour and discipline.* London: DfES

Training and Development Agency for Schools (TDA) (2007a) *Results of the newly qualified teacher survey 2007.* London: TDA

Training and Development Agency for Schools (TDA) (2007b) *Professional standards for teachers.* London: TDA

Visser, J (2000) *Managing behaviour in classrooms.* London: David Fulton

Westwood, P (2006) *Commonsense methods for children with special educational needs: strategies for the regular classroom.* Abingdon: RoutledgeFalmer

2
Top tips for teachers and why you need a wider understanding

Chapter objectives

By the end of this chapter you should be able to:

- **describe a range of behaviour management strategies;**
- **reflect upon the role of behaviour management strategies;**
- **begin to understand the complexities of achieving appropriate behaviour for learning.**

This chapter addresses the following Professional Standards for QTS:
Q2, Q10, Q31

Introduction

If only there was one book you could buy that could teach you everything you need to know to attain impeccable behaviour from children all day, every day. You could simply follow the rules laid out in the book: children would be perfectly behaved and learn everything and more that you taught them; Ofsted would give glowing reports; the government would not need to introduce any more initiatives; the author would be a billionaire and everyone could live happily ever after.

Unfortunately the situation is not that simple, largely because people are complex creatures and, as this book will increasingly demonstrate, factors affecting behaviour are multifaceted. As you are aware from the previous chapter, some of the Professional Standards for QTS specifically refer to your ability to 'manage' learners' behaviour. A brief exploration of your university library, an internet search or a scan of publishers' catalogues will quickly reveal the wide range of literature which helps you to manage behaviour. This chapter explores some of those techniques and strategies described in the literature and acknowledges the important role they play in managing behaviour.

Behaviour management strategies

Every school should have a behaviour policy which outlines their approach to managing behaviour, and it is essential that you know and understand its contents (Visser, 2000; Pollard et al., 2008, Cohen *et al.*, 2006). Of course, a policy is worthless if staff do not know what is in it, or do not apply it consistently. A good policy will detail the key strategies which staff should use, including the promotion of positive behaviour, in the course of their behaviour management.

The term 'behaviour management' is regularly used in the teaching profession, being found in policy, training, books and daily discourse in schools. You will find strategies detailed in a range of books: most books exploring how to be an effective teacher contain a chapter on managing behaviour, while others are entirely devoted to the topic. The key strategies contained in these books are summarised here to provide you with a background to the theory and practice that will help you on placement. However, it is misleading to think that a set of strategies used in isolation will prevent and resolve all behaviour problems. Behaviour management is not an 'add-on' to your teaching role: good behaviour and teaching/planning are very closely linked and cannot be separated (Elton Report 1989; Cohen *et al.*, 2006).

Prevention is better than cure

As Kyriacou (2001) states, the term 'prevention is better than cure' is particularly apt when dealing with misbehaviour. As you will become increasingly aware, a good teacher who maintains a well-ordered classroom 'makes it look easy.' However, as Visser (2000) states, good behaviour does not occur spontaneously. In fact, the teacher will have undertaken considerable preparation behind the scenes. Some of this will be highly visible, for example in the production of class rules which are often on display (Kyriacou, 2001). Rogers (1998) suggests that rules are best written in partnership with the children. They need to be framed positively where possible, for example 'walk' rather than 'don't run'. Rules should be simple, clear and achievable.

Crucially, staff need to regularly refer to and enforce them. 'Staff' refers to all in the school, not only teachers – children need to know that there are no 'weak links' who might ignore certain behaviours which other adults in the school will not tolerate. Consistent enforcement is not necessarily as easy as it sounds. On a wet afternoon when you and the children are tired and you are watching the clock tick towards home time, it can make for an easier life to stop enforcing the rules. These complications make it even more important for staff to be supportive of each other in their implementation of them.

Rules can play a vital role in the classroom because they offer children clear boundaries and set clear expectations. Of course, simply issuing a reminder of a rule such as *put your hand up if you would like to say something* does not immediately mean that the children will comply, because there are many more factors at play.

Self-presentation

When children do not respond to your reminders of the class rules, why might this be? One aspect to explore from the very first meeting with the children is how you are perceived by them.

CASE STUDY
Trainees' self-presentation
Howard is a university tutor who has observed large numbers of trainees. He is interested in how students present themselves to the class particularly in the initial stages. During the first placement he sees several in his cohort appearing slightly shy and nervous, while others are confident and outgoing, quickly demanding the children's attention. *Those who come across as quiet and a little reticent are storing up difficulties*, Howard explains. *If the children don't perceive the trainee to have any authority from day one, then they will respond accordingly – the children won't listen or comply with their requests quickly. It can be very difficult to gain the children's respect afterwards.*

A sense of authority does not imply a harsh, dictatorial manner. On the contrary, such an approach can have the opposite effect. Rogers (2006) suggests that confidence – not arrogant self-assurance – is the key. In part, this involves demonstrating relaxed body language, appearing composed and being pleasant. O'Flynn *et al.* (2003) also emphasise the importance of maintaining good eye contact with the children and note the importance of maintaining a calm and steady voice. This measured tone exudes confidence, in contrast to a high-pitched shrill which can display insecurity and loss of control. Confidence is something which develops with experience and is essential because when a teacher feels confident there is an implication that they expect the pupils to respond appropriately (O'Flynn *et al.*, 2003).

Of course, you may not be calm or confident in front of a class of children, particularly on your first meeting or when you are being observed. It is natural to be nervous, especially in your early placements, but it is important to appear confident. Acting is a key skill which you can develop with practice, as is becoming increasingly aware of the messages your body language is conveying. Asking a friend/fellow trainee to observe your interactions with children is a good way of investigating how others perceive you.

Be well prepared

In addition to growing through experience, confidence also comes, in part, from being well prepared (Rogers, 2006). The Elton Report (1989) noted that if teachers are effective classroom managers, then disruptive behaviour can be reduced. Thus, preparation for teaching is fundamental to achieving appropriate behaviour, ranging from creating a well-ordered and attractive physical environment to acknowledging the individual children's needs (Moyles, 2001).

Sound lesson preparation is central to preventing inappropriate behaviour (Cohen *et al.*, 2006). Clear aims and objectives, for example, give the children focus, while a variety of teaching strategies will engage their interest and cater for different learning styles. Moyles (2001) observes that much unacceptable behaviour can occur when pupils are unsure of what to do, or are bored with work which is unvaried. Pace of lessons is also important (Pollard *et al.*, 2008) – lessons which are too slow can cause children to lose interest and those which are too fast can fail to give adequate time to consolidate learning. Consequently, children's lack of engagement with the lesson can give rise to off-task or disruptive behaviour.

Being well prepared also includes consideration of how you will group the children during your lessons, to ensure that you have adequate differentiation, which has a strong bearing on behaviour (Cohen *et al.*, 2006). As a trainee you may be restricted to working with the teacher's groups, which can be advantageous as it provides continuity for the children. These groups may be a mixture of those based on ability, mixed ability, friendship or (less frequently) gender (Dean, 2000). If children are given purposeful tasks which are appropriate to their ability, they are more likely to be engaged in the work and not in misbehaviour. Work which is too difficult can lead to frustration, while work which is too easy can lead to boredom, with both situations being potential flashpoints for disruptive behaviour.

Transitions

Always be prepared for managing transitions, i.e. organising children as they move from one location to another. These may simply be: a move from the carpet area to desks; leaving the classroom at the end of a lesson; leading children in from the playground; or taking them into the hall for PE. Rogers (2006) emphasises the need for the teacher to have clear expectations of the children, so that they know what is expected of them. For example, if moving to their desks, children can be sent in groups for safety to avoid a rush, and need to know what they have to do once they arrive at their tables. You might appoint monitors to hand out books, and spare resources such as pencils should be easily available to the children to avoid unnecessary wastage of time.

Clear articulation of expectations regarding transitions is key to ensuring the children's appropriate behaviour. In turn, this behaviour is vital in guarding their safety while moving around the school or off site. For example, if you are sending children from a classroom to another part of the school, wait until all are quiet before you allow them to leave. Give clear instructions to walk quietly, and explain what they will need to do when they arrive at their destination. Always ensure that you position yourself so that you can see all of the children, which may mean that they need to stop part way, such as at the end of a corridor. If you are concerned that individuals are likely to behave irresponsibly, ensure that they are situated close to an adult and/or give them some responsibility, such as carrying something for you.

Rewards and sanctions

The Steer Report (2005, page 22) states:

> *Consistent experience of good teaching promotes good behaviour. But schools also need to have positive strategies for managing pupil behaviour that help pupils understand their school's expectations. These strategies must be underpinned by a clear range of rewards and sanctions...*

The school policy will outline the rewards and sanctions systems used in all classes, which you need to apply. Above, you learnt that consistency was necessary in enforcing rules, but consistency is also vital to managing behaviour across the school (Ofsted, 2005; Steer Report, 2005; Cohen *et al.*, 2006), and this applies to your role as a trainee too. If you follow the teacher's routines of offering house points for children who tidy their tables quickly at the end of a lesson, the children will know immediately what you expect of them.

REFLECTIVE TASK

What kinds of reward systems have you seen in schools? How did the children respond to them? Were some rewards more effective than others? How did the children respond to sanctions or to the threat of them?

Ethos

A final preventative measure to add to these practical preparations is the creation of an open, caring ethos in which all members of the school are valued and respected. The

Elton Report (1989) recognised the impact of a strong ethos. The report's authors observed differences in atmospheres in the schools which could not be explained by the home backgrounds of the pupils.

CASE STUDY
A warm ethos
Ranjit undertook a placement in an inner-city primary school which was set in an area of economic deprivation. He described his Year 3 class as a lively and noisy one, with many children having learning difficulties. From prior knowledge of the school he had presumed that he would be facing very challenging behaviour but his experience was quite different. From the moment he walked into the school, Ranjit felt very welcome. In the classroom he observed that the teacher had created a strong ethos of community. *Children appeared to be confident, felt safe in sharing their views and asking questions, were polite and helpful,* explained Ranjit. *It was so clear that the teacher knew all of the children really well and there was a wonderful nurturing atmosphere. Children enjoyed learning and any minor disruptions were dealt with in such a low-key manner that they were barely noticeable.*

Ravet (2007) emphasises the importance of a whole-school approach to developing and sustaining an ethos. This is not, she argues, simply about presenting a set of values in a policy that has little bearing on the daily workings of the school. Rather, a supportive ethos relates to an emotionally literate school where rights, responsibilities, open communication and collaboration are embedded in all areas of the school.

In a supportive environment, children can feel respected and appreciated, which increases positive behaviour. As a trainee, you will be making a contribution to the ethos of the school, despite the fact that you may be there for only a short time. In Chapter 4, when discussing relationships with others, the concepts of ethos and emotional literacy will be explored in more depth, together with a focus on your contribution to it.

Strategies for dealing with disruptive behaviour

Having put preventative measures in place, you will also need to have a repertoire of strategies to deal with different forms of disruptive behaviour when they occur. Rogers (2006) offers guidance on a range of techniques which are appropriate for various misbehaviours, which you can adapt to different situations. The following is a selection of those he suggests, which are placed in order of the degree of intrusion, beginning with the least.

- Tactical ignoring, where you deliberately ignore occasional incidents. You should never ignore repeatedly disruptive behaviour or those causing safety concerns.
- Non-verbal cueing, such as eye contact, which indicates your intention without spoken words.
- Incidental language. Rogers (2006, page 78) offers an example of *There's some litter on the floor and the bell is going to go soon*, which means *You know that I know that I'm encouraging you to pick it up*.
- Behavioural direction occurs when you direct a child referring to the expected behaviour, such as *Emma, hand up please*.
- Distraction/diversion. One tactic frequently used is to simply divert a child's attention by asking a question about their work to refocus them, or asking them to do a small job for you.

- Direct questions. Avoid open questions and ask a direct one such as *What is our rule for?* This indicates the responsibility of the child.
- 'Choice'/deferred consequences. This involves you stating the consequences of continued disruptive behaviour in the context of a 'choice'. For example, you might say to a child *If you choose not to give me your mobile phone, I will need to talk to you at playtime*.
- Command. Ultimately you may need to simply issue a command such as *John – stop that **now**.* Keep these short and to the point, and use them if an immediate stopping of the behaviour is required.

It is advisable to use commands sparingly, and only when the incident demands it, because issuing a command carries the danger that the child will not comply, which places you in a confrontational situation. If this occurs in front of other children, you are now in a compromising situation which can diminish your authority with the rest of the class. Moyles (2001) suggests counting to ten before responding, which gives you time to note what is happening and assess the situation.

Throughout your career, you will encounter incidents of high-level disruptive behaviour on occasions. Whatever the incident – whether it be defiant behaviour, inappropriate verbal comments, or violence against another child or staff member – you will have to respond to it. If the incident has appeared without warning, you will have to issue a command. As Rogers (2006) states, this command needs to be firm and clear. If other children are at risk, you can signal to them to move away and ask one to fetch other adult support. Rogers emphasises that you will also need a back-up plan in case the defiant pupil does not do as you tell them.

The school's policy will describe the agreed procedures that a staff member needs to follow in the event of a high-level disruptive incident. It might, for instance, involve a set number of warnings that you need to give to a child before sending them to a senior member of staff, and ultimately informing their parents/carers.

The fear of encountering a violent or abusive incident in the classroom is understandable, although the chance of it occurring in most primary classes is low. However, if it does arise, you are definitely not alone in dealing with it, and will have a strong network of support as detailed in Chapter 8.

O'Flynn *et al.* (2003) emphasise that it is important to maintain the relationship with a disruptive pupil as well as with the rest of the class. While dealing with the behaviour may entail administering the school's disciplinary code, it is also important to do so in a way that does not humiliate the child. Teachers in this situation frequently criticise, threaten, moralise, disapprove or isolate the child and this response, say O'Flynn *et al.* (2003), can lead to disaffection if they are the only responses used. It is important for the teacher to also reinforce, compliment, encourage, guide and question where appropriate to balance their sometimes negative responses.

'Top tips' and strategies: as easy as it sounds?

The advice on behaviour management given so far is straightforward. Policy-makers highlight good practice which is observed in schools and supported by research. As a trainee, NQT and also as a practising teacher, you will develop a range of strategies and become increasingly confident in managing behaviour. This development will occur provided that you take a reflective approach to your practice and engage with further training and developments in the field. While it is essential that you develop a range of strategies (as the

Standards Q10 and C38b require), you will discover that managing behaviour is not always as simple as it might sound, as Jess and Matthew in the following case study discovered while on placement.

CASE STUDY
But it doesn't always work

Jess and Matthew were on placement in Year 2 classes of a large urban school, and compared observations of their respective class teachers' approaches to behaviour management. Jess's class had a calm and co-operative ethos. When noise levels rose, the teacher would raise her hands in silence and the children would copy her, taking her action as a sign that they needed to talk more quietly. In Matthew's class, the teacher had a very different demeanour, easily frustrated by high noise levels and inattentive behaviour. She was prone to shouting over the children in order to bring noise levels down, but Matthew reported that this only seemed to increase the noise levels further. When Matthew began to teach this class, he tried to implement the raised-hand technique which Jess's teacher used. Matthew explained, *It had no effect at all – the children just didn't even look at me*.

When you are in a classroom full of children actively engaged in learning, with a teacher who is calm and uses a variety of effective strategies, behaviour management can look very simple. As Matthew discovered, though, simply implementing a strategy (or strategies) employed by others is not always as straightforward as it might seem. Why? Firstly, a good teacher will have undertaken considerable preparation 'behind the scenes' which would have prevented numerous incidents happening. As Haydn's (2007) research with trainees, teachers and teacher educators showed, the majority of his sample felt that their management had improved through preparation prior to teaching, not through tips and techniques for controlling children during lessons.

Secondly, children need to be taught what the strategies are and what they mean. In Matthew's class, the teacher had not used the raised-hand technique before, so the children did not know what it meant. Thirdly, context is also important in deciding which strategy to use. While this particular technique is designed to signal attention and quiet, it seems that the children had largely disregarded Matthew's presence. This could be because he had not presented himself with enough confidence on arrival, and/or because the children did not have a structured regime. However, that is not to say that a practitioner should disregard a strategy immediately if it is ineffective on its first use. Matthew was flexible and adapted it: *I made the strategy into a game to see how quickly they could stop talking, and that seemed to be the key with this class*, he explained.

PRACTICAL TASK PRACTICAL TASK PRACTICAL TASK PRACTICAL TASK PRACTICAL TASK

As a student you will be required to reflect critically upon all the aspects of training, including the theory and practice of behaviour management. Throughout your placements, you will need to reflect upon the strategies you have used, and consider their advantages and disadvantages and why they were or weren't effective. Keep this as an ongoing record throughout your training so that you can compare the effects of using the same strategies in different schools.

Strategy	What did you use it for?	Advantages	Disadvantages
Countdown from 10 to 1	To signal to children that I needed them to finish the work they were doing, and that they had 10 seconds in which to finish	In one class this worked very quickly. I gained the children's full attention in a couple of minutes. It worked because the children saw it as a game	This failed completely in another class because the children weren't familiar with the technique. They were also too noisy at the time, so many didn't hear the counting

Top tips... and the role of theory in behaviour

Authors of texts on behaviour management strategies take different approaches with regards to the amount of theory detailed. In the introduction to the second edition of *Getting the buggers to behave,* Sue Cowley states that her book is *accessible and easy to read. No academic theory – just lots of tips, advice and examples to show how the ideas... really work in practice.* She continues: *After all, how many of us, snowed under with reports to write and lessons to plan, have time to wade through endless theory?* (Cowley, 2001, page x). But theory *is* important, which the B4L approach acknowledges. Behaviour, as well as its relationship to learning, is complex in part because humans are complex and behaviour is learnt. Thus it is important that you understand aspects of theory which explore human behaviour, especially the cognitive, social and affective.

Behaviour management strategies are essential to your survival in the classroom and to meet the Standards, but your knowledge of them does need to be underpinned by theory. Haydn (2007, page 15) emphasises the complexity of managing classrooms, behaviour and learning, stating that this area of teaching is not straightforward or *susceptible to simple solutions or quick fixes.* The reality is, he continues, that even a good teacher in a good school can plan a lesson well but still have difficulty in managing the behaviour. Similarly, Weare (2004) argues that strategies for addressing behaviour need to go beyond management strategies, establishing clear expectations and administering punishments. The theory of emotional literacy is, she maintains, an integral part of understanding children's behaviour. This notion of emotional literacy is developed further in the following chapters, alongside relevant theories which show the complexity of understanding behaviour. These explorations will give you greater insight into why some children do not exhibit appropriate behaviour for learning, and highlight the multifaceted nature of the factors which influence children's behaviour.

A SUMMARY OF **KEY POINTS**

> Behaviour management is an integral part of all aspects of school life – sound preparation is essential to effective behaviour management.

> Knowing strategies for behaviour management and 'top tips' are vital for your successful behaviour management.

> Despite thorough preparation and a knowledge of a wide range of strategies, misbehaviour will still occur – there are no 'quick fixes'.

> Using behaviour management strategies and 'top tips' alone will not be sufficient to achieve high levels of good behaviour.

MOVING *ON* > > > > > > MOVING *ON* > > > > > > MOVING *ON*

Before reading this book, you will probably have undertaken a selection of the following activities to prepare yourself for managing children's behaviour on placement: attended lectures on behaviour, read books and articles on behaviour management, learnt different strategies to manage behaviour, observed teachers' practice and have begun to develop your own personal style in the classroom. During your induction year, you will be required to develop the range of strategies further, adapting as necessary, to promote the children's self-control and independence (C38b). You will need to focus on managing their behaviour in constructive ways by establishing a clear, positive framework for discipline which is in accordance with the school's policy (C38a). It is important that these strategies are up to date and that you can adapt and personalise them as appropriate to your pupils (C10).

The next chapter begins to explore the theory behind the B4L approach in more detail, beginning with the child's relationship with self.

FURTHER READING FURTHER READING **FURTHER READING** FURTHER READING

Cohen, L, Manion, L and Morrison, K (2006) *A guide to teaching practice.* Abingdon: Routledge. This book offers a very comprehensive guide to all aspects of your teaching practice. In particular, Chapter 15 provides a relatively concise but thorough overview of approaches to behaviour management, which is grounded in theory.

Rogers, B (2006) *Classroom behaviour: a practical guide to effective teaching, behaviour management and colleague support.* London: Paul Chapman. Rogers's book is easily accessible and provides a wide range of practical strategies which are supported with theory.

REFERENCES REFERENCES **REFERENCES** REFERENCES **REFERENCES** REFERENCES

Cohen, L, Manion, L and Morrison, K (2006) *A guide to teaching practice.* Abingdon: Routledge

Cowley, S (2001) *Getting the buggers to behave,* 2nd edition. London: Continuum

Dean, J (2000) *Organising teaching and learning in the primary school classroom.* London: Routledge

Elton Report (1989) *Discipline in schools.* London: HMSO

Haydn, T (2007) *Managing pupil behaviour. Key issues in teaching and learning.* Abingdon: Routledge

Kyriacou, C (2001) *Effective teaching in schools: theory and practice.* Cheltenham: Nelson Thornes

Moyles, J (2001) *Organising for learning in the primary classroom: a balanced approach to classroom management.* Buckingham: Open University Press

O'Flynn, S and Kennedy, H with MacGrath, M (2003) *Get their attention: how to gain the respect of students and thrive as a teacher.* London: David Fulton

Ofsted (2005) *Managing challenging behaviour.* London: Ofsted. Available from: www.ofsted.gov.uk/ Ofsted-home/Publications-and-research/Care/Childcare/Managing-challenging-behaviour/language/eng-GB, accessed 20 October 2008

Pollard, A, Collins, J, Simco, N, Swaffield, S, Warin, J, Warwick, P and Maddock, M (2008) *Reflective teaching: Evidence-informed professional practice*, 3rd edition. London: Continuum

Ravet, J (2007) *Are we listening? Making sense of classroom behaviour with pupils and parents.* Stoke on Trent: Trentham

Rogers, B (1998) *You know the fair rule. Strategies for making the hard job of discipline and behaviour management in school easier.* Harlow: Pearson Education

Rogers, B (2006) *Classroom behaviour: a practical guide to effective teaching, behaviour management and colleague support.* London: Paul Chapman

Steer Report (2005) *Learning behaviour: the report of the practitioners' group on school behaviour and discipline.* London: DfES

Weare, K (2004) *Developing the emotionally literate school.* London: Paul Chapman

Visser, J (2000) *Managing behaviour in classrooms.* London: David Fulton

3
Who am I? A child's sense of self

Chapter objectives

By the end of this chapter you should be able to:

- **reflect on your own sense of identity;**
- **understand the complexities of a child's sense of self;**
- **begin to understand how you can nurture a child's sense of self in school;**
- **recognise the importance of a child's sense of self in affecting their behaviour for learning.**

This chapter addresses the following Professional Standards for QTS:

Q1, Q2, Q3a, Q3b, Q4, Q7, Q14, Q15, Q30

Links to: spiritual, moral, social and cultural development (SMSC); personal, social and health and citizenship education (PSHCE); religious education (RE); Every Child Matters (ECM); social and emotional aspects of learning (SEAL).

Introduction

Each and every child is an individual. When they arrive in the classroom they bring with them a host of unseen factors which are contributing to their behaviour for learning. When seeking to ensure positive behaviour for learning, your immediate thoughts may be focused on the need for engaging, well-prepared lessons and an attractive classroom environment. While these are important, this chapter will demonstrate how the child's sense of self also plays a vital role in affecting their behaviour for learning. This relationship cannot be seen in isolation from those with other people and curriculum, so it is important that this chapter is read in conjunction with Chapters 4 and 5, which have areas of overlap.

Identity

You will often hear new parents exclaiming how their young babies and toddlers quickly exhibit their own personality traits, which are often quite distinct from those of their siblings. As children grow, their sense of self-awareness and of identity develops quickly as they explore their own feelings, test boundaries, engage in the world and socialise with others. You will have noticed through your observations made on placement and through your relationships with them just how individual children are. No two children are the same, just as no two adults are the same. In the classroom, from the Early Years onwards, teachers encourage children to explore their own identity, through discussions about their feelings, their relationships and reflection on their actions. But before teachers do this, it is important that they too have a good understanding of their own sense of identity.

PRACTICAL TASK PRACTICAL TASK PRACTICAL TASK PRACTICAL TASK PRACTICAL TASK

Who are you?

Imagine that a stranger has just asked you to tell them about yourself. Take a few moments to complete the table below to describe yourself to them. Some examples are given for you.

Your 'titles'	Your academic skills	Positive personal attributes	Negative personal attributes	General temperament
e.g. son/ daughter, student, friend	e.g. artist, mathematician	e.g. thoughtful, good listener, organised	e.g. selfish, unreliable, judgemental	e.g. calm, excitable, changeable

This table is the first step in articulating your identity. Trainees often struggle to complete the positive personal attributes box, while they regularly comment that they could fill the negative personal attributes column several times over. Such a response is very interesting and often comes as a surprise to them, perhaps highlighting how little we as adults compliment each other in the course of daily life. If you have struggled to identify your positive traits, ask a friend to list what they perceive them to be. To do so is a valuable exercise in exploring how we see ourselves compared with how others see us – and a lesson to bear in mind when you interact with children who may have a different view of themselves compared with how you perceive them.

REFLECTIVE TASK

Now reflect further on what you have written so far, and add anything which might not fall into the categories given. For example, you might refer to your cultural or religious identity. Finally, consider your responses in relation to your peers. If you were to think of your friends, you might also be able to apply many of these descriptions to them too. Yet we are all very different from each other, even if we share similar personality traits and academic talents... so what is it that makes you YOU?

To answer this last question, you may need to make a much deeper exploration. You might, for example, consider your fundamental beliefs about the world.

- Do you think the world is a supportive, nurturing place or a hostile one full of corruption?
- Do successful people achieve their aims through hard work and talent, or through luck or knowing the right people?
- Does society value the conformist members or the rebels?
- Do you have strong political beliefs?
- What drives your beliefs about life – is it a religious stance, a spiritual approach, or an atheistic one?
- What do you value most in the world?

These questions go some way to exploring who you are – how you define yourself from different perspectives. This exercise, particularly towards the end, may have been a little uncomfortable, particularly as our society does not always encourage such introspection. However, self-reflection is an important part of your professional development, and is explored in depth in Chapter 9 in relation to your progression with understanding the factors affecting behaviour. For now, reflect upon your own self-concept. You might think that the latter questions in this section are rather philosophical in nature and have little to do with children or behaviour, but a sense of self is highly appropriate to children – and to their behaviour for learning – as the rest of this chapter will illustrate.

Children's identity

As the above tasks demonstrated, the articulation of our identity is not always simple but it is important to realise that a child's sense of identity can be strong, even if they cannot articulate it clearly either. Personal, social, health and citizenship education (PSHCE), which crosses subject boundaries, addresses the notion of self and provides children with the opportunities to reflect upon themselves. Although PSHCE is non-statutory, most schools will have programmes in place which cover at least some of the aspects of the guidance. These include, at Key Stage 1, children learning about themselves as developing individuals, including recognising what they like and dislike, thinking about themselves and identifying their feelings. At Key Stage 2, children may be asked to discuss and write about their view, identify how people's emotions change during puberty, and to recognise their worth as individuals.

Similarly, spiritual, moral, social and cultural development (SMSC), which is statutory and cross-curricular, requires teachers to help children explore and develop aspects of themselves.

Eaude (2008) explores SMSC in depth and provides a thorough overview of the requirements for schools in this area. In the course of this and the next two chapters, I draw on those elements of SMSC which are particularly relevant to behaviour, beginning with spiritual development, which is perhaps the theme which teachers and trainees are least confident about. As Eaude (2008) states, the 'spiritual' is probably the most difficult of the four elements of SMSC to define. However, acknowledging teachers' uncertainty, Ofsted (2004, page 12) produced a guidance document which aims to clarify definitions for them. Part of their definition reads *[spiritual development is] the development of a sense of identity, self-worth, personal insight, meaning and purpose.* While Ofsted's advice has faced critique, largely because the term 'spiritual' tends to defy definition, the booklet does offer you some practical advice on what they look for in their inspections of SMSC. Given that it is easier to describe the spiritual than define it, let's take the notion of identity and explore what theorists have written on that topic.

A key component of that description of spirituality is the child's journey to develop a sense of self. Elsewhere (Adams *et al.*, 2008), it is argued that finding a sense of self is an essential part of childhood and an aspect of spirituality. Children naturally explore their place in the world – their relationships, what is meaningful to them, how they are connected to the world and who they are. Such explorations are essential to establishing an outlook on the world and to sensing how they fit in. Their responses will affect the choices they make in life.

Spiritual experiences in childhood can make a major impact upon a sense of identity but this realm of children's lives may be hidden from you. This is largely due to cultural factors in the West which downplay the importance of spiritual experience: Hay (1985) warns that there is a suspicion of the spiritual in British society, and a reluctance to talk about matters of personal religious and spiritual beliefs. Yet studies by researchers show that children have spiritual experiences, some of which make a significant and lasting impact upon them.

RESEARCH SUMMARY RESEARCH SUMMARY **RESEARCH SUMMARY** RESEARCH SUMMARY

Children's spiritual lives

Champagne (2001) shows how children in the Early Years can become completely engaged in moments of awe and wonder. She describes how a two-and-a-half-year-old girl found a feather floating on the tide and became fascinated by it, exploring how it moved on the tide for almost half an hour. Hart (2003) describes how some children see people who have died or see auras around people, while I explore the impact of significant dreams on children's spiritual lives (see Adams, 2003). Hay and Nye (2006, page 109) describe spirituality as involving 'relational consciousness' because it involves a person's sense of connectedness or relationships. One key category of spiritual experience is 'child self-consciousness' – when spirituality is expressed in the context of the child's sense of relationship with themselves. Hay and Nye offer an example of Jenny, a ten-year-old girl, who focused on existential questions such as *Why am I here?* and had a vivid sense of self-consciousness, feeling that sometimes she would 'pop out' of her own body (Hay and Nye, 2006, page 117). Hyde (2008) also emphasises the importance of relationships in children's spiritual lives, and argues that in their spiritual questing they seek ways of connecting to self (and others).

Although SMSC is cross-curricular, spiritual and moral development also have a particularly strong connection with RE (even though 'spiritual' is not synonymous with 'religious'). Although not part of the National Curriculum, RE is a subject required by law, initially by the Education Act of 1944 when it was termed 'religious instruction'. The Education Reform Act of 1988 continued its legal status but renamed it 'religious education'. There is no single curriculum – instead, there is a variety of agreed syllabi which outline what each school (according to its status and geographical location) need to cover. Each will, however, contain broadly similar material, which will include children's reflection upon inner lives, beliefs and matters of identity.

PRACTICAL TASK PRACTICAL TASK **PRACTICAL TASK** PRACTICAL TASK **PRACTICAL TASK**

Check your school's agreed syllabus for the exact details of what needs to be taught. Look for themes in which children are asked to reflect on religious and spiritual feelings and experiences, identify matters of personal importance and contemplate themselves, their uniqueness, and their place in a community.

It may be that you included religious beliefs in the exploration of your own identity at the beginning of this chapter. For many, religion is a shaping force in identity, and religious and/ or spiritual experiences which occur in childhood can be particularly significant. In his seminal work on children's religious experience, Robinson (1977) gathered data from adults and found that many religious experiences had occurred during their childhood years. These experiences remained vivid memories for the correspondents. In particular, they referred to the experiences as having great personal significance when contemplating issues of identity and meaning in life.

So, a key theme of spiritual development is the journey to self-understanding. Social, cultural and moral development also have close links. We often define ourselves, in part, by our cultural upbringing. Two friends of mine would always tease each other as Johan, a Belgian, defined himself as European while Jane defined herself as English and would never think to use the term 'European' to describe herself. Often our self-perceptions, morals, views about the world and our values are influenced by our cultural norms.

> **REFLECTIVE TASK**
>
> Return to the identity tasks at the beginning of this chapter. Reflect on each of your answers: how many of these have been influenced by the culture within which you were raised? If you had grown up in a different country with a different culture, might some of your answers differ?

As Eaude (2008) states, our cultural development, like our social and moral development, can be seen in two ways – as internal to the person, and as external. The internal includes our levels of self-esteem or self-belief, while the external can encompass levels of understanding of other cultures which can manifest in bullying or racism. As with moral development, our responses can depend on both habit and conscious choice. Eaude offers the example of bullying, stating that it is less likely to happen in a culture which sees it as unacceptable, but children also need to be given the tools to reflect upon what is similar and what is different about themselves compared with others; to reflect on what they believe is appropriate behaviour or inappropriate behaviour.

Identity – self-awareness and managing feelings

When you help children to understand themselves, a key focus is on exploring and learning to manage feelings and emotions. Daniel Goleman's (1996) notion of emotional intelligence (EI) has made a significant contribution to this area in recent years. Goleman (1996) works on the theory expounded by Howard Gardner (1983) that intelligence is not fixed and has many different components. It is argued that by being aware of our own emotional responses and trusting them, we are able to understand and manage our feelings more effectively. The concept of EI is explored in more detail in the next chapter, but for now, how can you address this aspect of children's development in the classroom?

There are many programmes available which are focused on children's feelings. One example is the packs offered by SEAL – the Social and Emotional Aspects of Learning – which offer schools a wide range of activities and ideas which can contribute to a child's developing sense of self. SEAL argues that there are five aspects of social and emotional learning. These include self-awareness and managing feelings (as well as motivation, empathy and social skills). SEAL demands a whole-school commitment to developing personal and emotional learning and to providing a nurturing ethos in which children feel safe to explore their relationship with self.

What connections does a sense of identity have with behaviour for learning? Such explorations into inner worlds are essential for children to establish an outlook on the outer world and to sense how they fit in. Their responses will affect the choices in life they make, including their behaviours. For example, children (as well as teenagers and adults) may engage in risky behaviours for a variety of reasons which can include seeking excitement or deliberate attempts to disobey authority. But sometimes these reasons include a desire or need to assert their independence or identity (Adams *et al.*, 2008).

When a child feels anonymous or that they have lost their sense of personal identity, Long (2000, page 251) suggests that a process of 'deindividuation' might have occurred. Secondary school pupils are more exposed to this risk than primary children because they are in large classes with several teachers throughout a week. As a primary teacher you will thus have an advantage in being able to know your pupils on a more personal level because you will spend considerably more time with them. However, the process of deindividuation can be a perceived one; a teacher may believe that they acknowledge and affirm each child in their class but if a child perceives that they are being overlooked or misunderstood, they can feel anonymous in relation to their peers. Long (2000) suggests that one consequence of feeling anonymous is a decreased sense of responsibility and a tendency to join in with class misbehaviour. It is thus important that you not only develop affirming relationships with the children quickly – a theme developed further in the next chapter – but also assist them in developing a strong sense of identity.

Self-efficacy

The term 'identity' is more complex than it might first appear, and we now need to examine other components which contribute to a child's sense of self, and also relate to behaviour for learning. Self-efficacy is a key trait. Self-efficacy can be described as a person's judgement of their ability to execute a behaviour which is necessary to produce certain outcomes (EPPI, 2004). The notion developed from the work of Bandura (1986), who writes from a social constructivist approach. He argues that self-efficacy relates to our perceptions of our ability to perform an academic task. Such perceptions are not created in isolation from others because major influences include feedback from teachers on efforts, and comparisons with peers' achievements. Our previous achievements also make an impact on our perception of our own ability and can also vary according to the tasks we are undertaking. For example, regularly low marks in science can lead a child to believe that they have low scientific ability.

CASE STUDY

Well behaved – in some lessons but not others!

Koreena found number work in maths particularly difficult and became frustrated. She began to develop avoidance strategies in maths lessons, finding excuses to wander around the room in search of pencils or rubbers. Yet her behaviour for learning was quite different in other curriculum areas which she was more comfortable with. Her perceptions of her differing abilities were paramount in determining how her behaviour for learning manifested.

The second case study explores an apparently simple case of a boy who believed that he had the ability to achieve in swimming and adopted positive behaviour to achieve his goal. However, it also demonstrates how such a situation is more complex than it may first appear.

> ### CASE STUDY
> **I want to swim like my friends can**
> John was a six-year-old who had struggled to learn to swim, managing only three or four strokes without floats or armbands. He was aware that his classmates were all able to swim unaided further than him, and was determined to catch up with them. John was also aware that he had made considerable progress in the last month, by swimming unaided for the first time. John's teacher was constantly telling him that he needed to concentrate and listen to her instructions more carefully; he had a lively disposition and a short concentration span, and spent considerable time in lessons chatting to friends. John knew that if he did listen a little more carefully, he would strengthen his chances of swimming further and over the course of the next few lessons he became increasingly focused on the teacher's guidance and earned his five-metre swimming badge.

Self-esteem

There was more to John's situation than simply listening to his teacher and behaving as she had asked because he wanted to swim as well as his friends. Other factors were also in play. One key factor, which is fundamental to a child's relationship with self and impacts upon behaviour for learning, is self-esteem – something which John had good levels of. Self-esteem refers to a person's general sense of worth (Muijs and Reynolds, 2001) and is fundamental to our success in learning, as both children and adults.

Abraham Maslow (1954) saw esteem as a vital human need. He developed a hierarchy of needs, depicted in Figure 3.1 below.

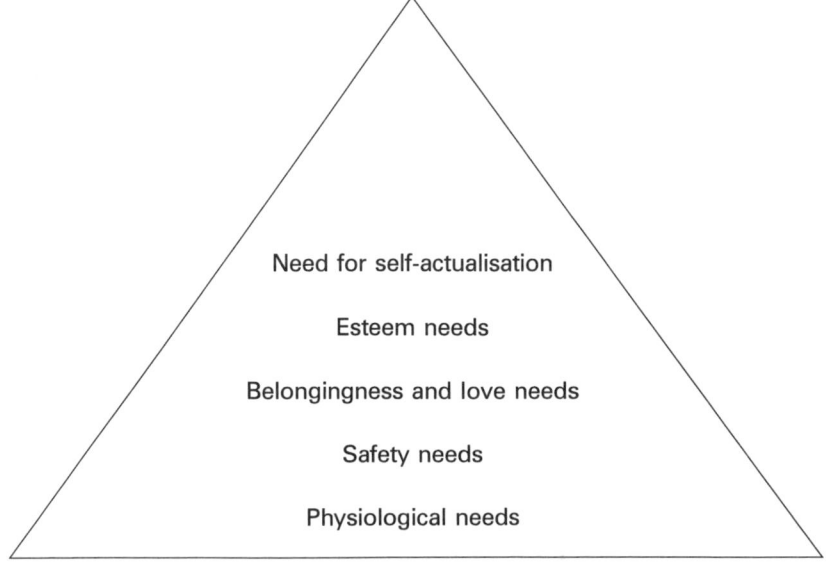

Figure 3.1 Maslow's hierarchy of needs

According to his theory, at the most basic levels are physiological needs such as food, water and warmth. Once those have been satisfied, safety needs, such as attaining security, come into play. These are followed by the need to belong, have affection and feel love, and once attained, people then seek to satisfy the esteem needs. Maslow maintained that people need a high self-evaluation, self-respect, self-esteem and to also gain the esteem of others. In essence, there is a desire for achievement and competence together with a need to have status, prestige, recognition or appreciation. If all of these needs have been met, people might then seek self-actualisation. This refers to a desire for self-fulfilment – to become everything that they are capable of becoming.

CASE STUDY
A tale of two children

Adam and Emily were nine-year-old classmates. Adam met with success at every academic subject at school. With a reading age of 14 he was significantly ahead of his peers and his mathematical abilities were also beyond those of many of the older children in his school. Adam was a sociable boy and was popular but was not particularly adept at sporting activities or art. Emily had average ability overall but had particular difficulties with literacy and was achieving below the expected standards for her age despite persevering.

Adam and Emily's behaviour for learning differed. Adam's self-esteem was lower than Emily's, despite his higher achievements. The fact that he did not accomplish well in sport or art was difficult for him to come to terms with and in those lessons he would not focus, and would constantly distract others. This behaviour stemmed largely from a desire to mask his inability in those curriculum areas – while in theory his self-esteem should have been high, he could not manage what he perceived to be failure, and this damaged his self-esteem. As Dweck (2000) argues, while it might be natural to assume that children with the highest ability are most likely to relish a challenge and persevere if they don't meet with success, the opposite can be true. For these children, a fear of failure can be intense and when faced with potential failure, they may give up.

Emily's situation was different. She had a cheerful, optimistic disposition and was determined to succeed to the best of her ability. *I know I'm not the cleverest in the class*, she said, *but if I do my best that's all I can do. And no one can be good at everything!* Emily had a strong sense of identity and her self-esteem was relatively high. Consequently, she exhibited positive behaviour for learning.

While self-esteem does not develop in isolation from relationships with others, there are activities you can undertake in the classroom to develop children's self-esteem. As we saw in the previous chapter, praise is an important part of the adult's role. You will know yourself how good it feels when you are complimented about your lesson preparation, your teaching, or a well-written assignment. Praise can spur us on to achieve further – it alerts us that others have recognised our talents, and gives us self-belief. It is, however, important that any praise given is sincere and realistic (Muijs and Reynolds, 2001). Children will quickly become aware that praise which is dished out in large spoonfuls with little substance is in fact meaningless.

A variety of activities can be undertaken in schools to enhance children's self-esteem. A popular activity for Key Stage 1 and Key Stage 2 children is circle time, developed by Jenny Mosley, which links particularly well to PSHCE. Children sit in a circle with an adult and discuss ideas, or contribute on a given theme with the adult taking the role of facilitator. Proponents claim that activities can aid children's self-confidence, improve their self-esteem and offer opportunities to identify their own needs.

One of the values which underpins quality circle time is a respect for self. This can help children to develop self-discipline, feel emotionally safe and enhance self-esteem if a good sanctions system is embedded within it. Mosley (1996) suggests that the use of circle time in a school should result in a whole-school policy on self-esteem. In turn, this promotion of social development can, says Mosley (1998), make a positive impact upon bullying. She argues that many emotional and behavioural problems in school are a result of unmet needs, particularly in environments where there are no proactive listening systems.

However, despite its popularity among teachers, circle time has met with criticism. Revell (2004) challenges some of the assumptions upon which circle time is based, arguing that in reality it legitimises various emotional and behavioural responses while simultaneously undermining others. She also argues that there has been no research undertaken to prove the claims that circle time improves self-esteem. Finally, Revell (2004) suggests that the teacher who facilitates is actually taking the role of a therapist – a role which is not within the remit of a teacher.

You may have seen circle time in action in schools, and may have led sessions your-selves. Further reading about its rationale, and experience of sessions, will enable you to form your own judgements about its success as a method. For now, though, consider the following questions.

REFLECTIVE TASK

- Do you think that a teacher has a responsibility to raise children's self-esteem?
- Can a teacher raise levels of self-esteem without becoming a therapist or counsellor?
- Does a teacher need to have high levels of self-esteem before they can raise children's?

What happens when self-esteem is low? Maslow (1954) argued that when self-esteem needs are not satisfied, feelings of inferiority and helplessness can occur. If we apply this idea to pupils, it is possible that negative attitudes towards learning might arise. Children may feel that they are not as able as their peers, and so feel intimidated by others' achievements in the classroom. This may manifest as lack of effort in their own work, or as disruptive behaviour during lessons.

Self-confidence

The Every Child Matters agenda recognises the value of self-confidence and lists the aim *develop self-confidence* under its 'Make a positive contribution' outcome (DfES, 2004). Self-confidence has links to self-esteem. Children who are confident, like Emily, described in the case study above, also usually have a strong sense of self. They know who they are, know what their talents are and what their weaknesses are, and are accepting of them. However, it is not necessarily the case that children with high levels of confidence will naturally approach all future tasks with assurance and persistence. Confidence tends to be a good predictor of academic success, but Dweck (2000) argues that confidence does not always help students when they face difficulty. While it is intuitive to believe that confident students will be able to face new challenges, she maintains it is not necessarily the case. As noted above, for some children, a fear of failure can highlight the fragility of the confidence.

REFLECTIVE TASK

- How does self-confidence affect your behaviour for learning?
- How can you boost a child's sense of self-confidence?
- Is offering praise enough?
- What is the role of planning in developing children's self-confidence?

Motivation

Closely linked to identity, self-efficacy, self-esteem and self-confidence is motivation. Long (2000, page 104) states that *the best way of understanding motivation is to see it not as a single quality but rather as a process that comes into play whenever we are involved in an activity*. Motivation does not simply relate to levels of involvement in an activity but also the reasons for its direction and it can vary from situation to situation. Long (2000) offers the example of a child who may seem lacking in motivation at school, rarely seeming committed to any topics studied. Yet that same child might be highly motivated at home when spending considerable time and energy playing on a complex computer game.

Motivation can come from different sources, and there are both intrinsic and extrinsic motivators. In the former, a person carries out a task for its own sake. Examples include a child who plays football because they derive enjoyment from it, or a young child eagerly experimenting with paints who is doing so through a natural desire to learn and experiment. In contrast, extrinsic motivators are external to the individual. These often include rewards and in the school context can relate to children completing work or behaving well because there is a reward waiting for them. While these two motivators are strong influences, it would be too simplistic to attribute all our motivating behaviours to them. As Long (2000) observes, the sense of self is an immediate and powerful explanation for academic motivation, as this chapter has already shown. It is important that in your exploration of behaviour for learning in relation to sense of self, you remain alert to the interaction of all of these factors. In Chapter 1, you undertook a short reflective task on your levels of motivation on your ITT course. This time, contemplate the links between your motivation levels and the other components of your relationship with self.

REFLECTIVE TASK

Focus again on your own levels of motivation train as a teacher. How are your levels of motivation linked to the other components of your identity? What are the links with your levels of self-efficacy, self-esteem and self-confidence?

Motivation, like the other components of identity detailed in this chapter, can impact upon a child's behaviour for learning. A highly motivated child determined to succeed is likely to be focused on their task. In contrast, a less motivated child is more likely to be distracted and less concerned about achieving quality in their work. Motivation, however, does not operate in isolation – a motivated child may have low self-confidence, for example, and fear failure.

As a trainee you will have encountered children who may be described as motivated and unmotivated. Motivating the latter can be a challenging task. Extrinsic rewards are commonly resorted to but can be superficial and convey the wrong message if over-reliance upon them occurs; children may adopt more conscientious approaches to learning but you need to ensure that they are not doing so just to get a reward.

A sense of self is thus inherently multifaceted and is considerably more complex than simply being described by our personality traits. It is essential to recognise all of the elements which compose our sense of self and their origins and influences. Over time, you will need to gain a more complete understanding of a child and their sense of identity. Doing so will give you insight and understanding into their attitudes towards learning.

A SUMMARY OF **KEY POINTS**

> **A relationship with self consists of various, interlinked components. These include identity, self-efficacy, self-esteem, self-confidence and motivation.**

> **Children's relationship with themselves can have a significant effect upon their behaviour for learning.**

> **Different aspects of the curriculum enable teachers to address issues of self in a variety of ways.**

MOVING *ON* > > > > > > MOVING *ON* > > > > > > MOVING *ON*

This chapter has given you insight into the importance of a child's relationship with self in relation to behaviour for learning, and has also highlighted the complexities of that relationship. In your induction year you will have the time to build relationships with the children in your class to a deeper level than you have been able to during short placements. Ensure that you take that time to understand each child and to nurture their relationship with self throughout the curriculum (C16). You will further develop your understanding of how children's well-being is affected by a range of factors including the social, religious and cultural (C18). Having your own teaching space will enable you to establish a purposeful and safe learning environment, in which you can help children feel sufficiently confident to make an active contribution to their learning and to the school (C37a). At the same time, you can help to promote their self-control and independent thought, developing their social, emotional and behavioural skills (C39).

A child's sense of self does not, of course, develop in isolation. The next chapter explores the role of children's relationships with others which can have a profound effect upon their sense of self and on their behaviour for learning.

FURTHER READING FURTHER READING **FURTHER READING** FURTHER READING

Dweck, C (2000) *Self-theories: their role in motivation, personality and development.* Philadelphia: Psychology Press. This book provides a detailed examination of theoretical perspectives.

Eaude, T (2008) *Children's spiritual, moral, social and cultural development – primary and early years.* Exeter: Learning Matters. A very clear and detailed overview of the components of SMSC and their complexities, many of which impinge on children's sense of self.

EPPI Centre (2004) *A systematic review of how theories explain learning behaviour in school contexts.* You can download the report from www.behaviour4learning.ac.uk

Ofsted (2004) *Promoting and evaluating pupils' spiritual, moral, social and cultural development.* London: Ofsted. This publication offers teachers guidance on what Ofsted looks for in these areas. You can identify the themes which relate to sense of self.

SEAL – Social and Emotional Aspects of Learning. See the Social, Emotional and Behavioural Skills website: www.teachernet.gov.uk/teachingandlearning/socialandpastoral/seal_learning/ accessed 20 October 2008

REFERENCES REFERENCES **REFERENCES** REFERENCES **REFERENCES** REFERENCES

Adams, K (2003) Children's dreams: an exploration of Jung's concept of big dreams. *International Journal of Children's Spirituality,* 8 (2): 105–14

Adams, K, Hyde, B and Woolley, R (2008) *The spiritual dimension of childhood.* London: Jessica Kingsley

Bandura, A (1986) *Social foundations of thought and action: a social cognitive theory.* Englewood Cliffs, N.J: Prentice Hall

Champagne, E (2001) Listening to . . . listening for . . . : A theological reflection on spirituality in early childhood. In J Erricker, C Ota and C Erricker (eds) *Spiritual education. Cultural, religious and social differences, new perspectives for the 21st century.* Brighton: Sussex Academic

DfES (2004) *Every Child Matters: change for children.* London: DfES

Dweck, C (2000) *Self-theories: their role in motivation, personality and development.* Philadelphia: Psychology Press

Eaude, T (2008) *Children's spiritual, moral, social and cultural development – primary and early years.* Exeter: Learning Matters

EPPI (2004) *A systematic review of how theories explain learning behaviour in school contexts.* Available from: www.behaviour4learning.ac.uk, accessed 5 January 2008

Gardner, H (1983) *Frames of mind: the theory of multiple intelligence.* New York: Basic Books

Goleman, D (1996) *Emotional intelligence. Why it can matter more than IQ.* London: Bloomsbury

Hart, T (2003) *The secret spiritual world of children.* Maui: Inner Ocean

Hay, D (1985) Suspicion of the spiritual: teaching religion in a world of secular experience. *British Journal of Religious Education,* 7 (3): 40–147

Hay, D and Nye, R (2006) *The spirit of the child.* London: Jessica Kingsley

Hyde, B (2008) *Children and spirituality: searching for meaning and connectedness.* London: Jessica Kingsley

Long, M (2000) *The psychology of education.* London: RoutledgeFalmer

Maslow, A (1954) *Motivation and personality.* New York: Harper and Row

Mosley, J (1996) *Turn your school around.* Wisbech: LDA

Mosley, J (1998) *More quality circle time – evaluating your practice and developing creativity within the whole school quality circle time model,* volume 2. Wisbech: LDA

Muijs, D and Reynolds, D (2001) *Effective teaching – evidence and practice.* London: Paul Chapman Publishing

Ofsted (2004) *Promoting and evaluating pupils' spiritual, moral, social and cultural development.* London: Ofsted

Revell, L (2004) Circle time, in D Hayes (2004) *The RoutledgeFalmer guide to key debates in education,* pp55–9. London: RoutledgeFalmer

Robinson, E (1977) *The original vision, a study of the religious experience of childhood.* Oxford: The Religious Experience Unit

4
Interactions:
children's relationships with others

Chapter objectives

By the end of this chapter you should be able to:

- **understand the importance of children's relationships to others in influencing behaviour for learning;**
- **be aware of the effects of different relationships on behaviour for learning.**

This chapter addresses the following Professional Standards for QTS:

Q1, Q4, Q5, Q6, Q31

Links to: spiritual, moral, social and cultural development (SMSC); personal, social and health and citizenship education (PSHCE); Every Child Matters (ECM); Early Years Foundation Stage (EYFS); social and emotional aspects of learning (SEAL); the Extended Schools initiative.

Introduction

People are, by nature, social creatures and so relationships with others are an integral part of our lives. With regards to behaviour for learning, relationships are also fundamental, particularly given that school learning is situated in group contexts. While the previous chapter has shown the importance of the child's relationship with self, this chapter explores how relationships with others affect children's behaviour for learning – various relationships in the school, those at home and also in the wider community. Firstly, the generic characteristics of effective relationships are considered through an examination of emotional literacy in education. Secondly, key relationships which children are engaged in are explored in the context of their behaviour.

The role of relationships

Humans are social creatures. While some people can be described as less sociable than others, we all need social contact. Importantly, the quality of that social contact can make lasting impressions on us. Damaging interactions, such as being bullied or persistently ignored in childhood, can damage self-esteem and confidence for many years. Conversely, nurturing interactions can build self-esteem and confidence, empowering children to become independent thinkers who can also work collaboratively and have strong social and emotional skills.

Naturally, our social development is complex, in part because our relationships with people, from a young age, are wide ranging in number, quality and in type. As a child we interact with parents/carers, siblings, other relatives, babysitters, strangers, staff at school, people in the local community from shopkeepers to bus drivers to neighbours, friends, friends' siblings and children we don't particularly like. Some of these interactions are regular, some are fleeting, some are deep, some are very superficial – but all have the potential to influence us in different ways.

In order to function in society, children need to develop social and emotional skills. These allow them to form friendships and other personal and professional relationships, empowering them to work collaboratively, negotiate aspects of life, share opinions, solve problems, develop independence and become responsible citizens, among many other things. The emphasis on our social nature is strong in educational policy. The Early Years Foundation Stage (EYFS) aims to help young children achieve the five areas of the ECM agenda (be healthy, stay safe, enjoy and achieve, make a positive contribution and achieve economic well-being). EYFS emphasises the importance of relationships, identifying 'positive relationships' as one of four complementary themes, together with 'a unique child', 'enabling environments' and 'learning and development' (DCSF, 2008, page 8).

As seen earlier, the National Curriculum's emphasis on SMSC and PSHCE ensures that the focus on social development is continued as children grow older. The development of their social skills is intertwined with moral, social and spiritual development, as well as citizenship. This can be achieved in a variety of ways, including developing emotional literacy, implementing programmes such as SEAL, and enabling sound relationships throughout the school.

Emotionally literate schools

The value of emotional intelligence, and its importance in relationships in schools, is increasingly being recognised. As the previous chapter briefly stated, Goleman (2004) developed Howard Gardner's (1983) theory that intelligence is not fixed but has many different components. Goleman (2004) draws on the work of Salovey and Mayer (1990), who offered an initial definition of emotional intelligence. Emotional intelligence involves five key domains.

- knowing one's emotions – being self aware and recognising emotions as they occur;
- managing emotions – being able to manage feelings in an appropriate manner;
- motivating oneself – the ability to have self-control over emotions;
- recognising emotions in others – empathy;
- handling relationships – managing emotions in others is a key skill in handling effective relationships.

If the basic principles of emotional intelligence are applied to schools, these schools are said to be emotionally literate. Weare (2004) shows how an emotionally literate school is in part characterised by its understanding of social situations and its ability to form relationships. She argues that forming attachments to others, having empathy for them, communicating and responding effectively and managing relationships are some of the key features of such a school. With explicit reference to behaviour, Weare (2004, page 67) suggests that schools need to understand the notion that *behaviour has a meaning, or at least a pay-off and . . . we need to work to uncover and understand the meanings or rewards that are stemming from that behaviour.* In particular, it is the emotional origins and outcomes that we need to understand. In order to achieve this, Weare suggests, it is necessary for a school to comprehend the links between behaviour, learning and emotion.

In some cases, a school might choose to implement a programme which focuses on developing social and emotional skills. In the USA, these have included Head Start, which is a preschool programme, and the Resolving Conflict Creatively Program. The latter, implemented in several hundred US schools, offers conflict-resolution strategies in the playground to prevent the escalation of violence (Goleman, 2004). In the UK you will encounter various programmes, with SEAL – the Social and Emotional Aspects of Learning – being one of the most common. In the previous chapter you learnt that SEAL addresses five aspects of social and emotional learning: self-awareness, managing feelings, motivation, empathy and social skills.

These five components link explicitly with SMSC and PSHCE. As SEAL states, these five aspects of learning are crucial in primary schools because they underlie almost every aspect of people's lives, enable effective learning, facilitate relationships and allow people to become responsible citizens. The SEAL packs provide frameworks for whole-curriculum approaches, lesson ideas and assembly materials.

However, for a school to develop emotional literacy, it is essential that all adults have a shared understanding of the concept and are committed to it. As Goleman (2004) observes, teachers need to be comfortable talking about feelings, which of course not all are. For schools that choose to adopt an approach based on emotionally literacy, a staff development course would be needed to ensure that all had a full understanding of the concept and a shared vision as to how it would work across the school.

Empathy has long been recognised as a quality which is essential to positive relationships. Psychologist Carl Rogers (1983) argued that a teacher's empathy with children is essential to their learning and to their personal growth, as they find someone who understands them, and does not seek to analyse or judge them. In a school setting, an empathic approach can thus give the children the confidence to share their thoughts and feelings (in PSHCE or RE, for example) because they know that their teacher will value what they say, understand them and not judge them. This environment will contribute to a strong ethos which in turn will positively influence behaviour, and strengthen children's relationships with others. The following sections explore these relationships more fully.

Children's relationships with the teacher

Within the school, children are engaged in a variety of relationships, which have different impacts and influences on their behaviour. Within the primary school, the relationship with the teacher is of fundamental importance, especially given that children spend most, if not all, of their week with that same teacher. But what defines a 'good' relationship between pupil and teacher?

RESEARCH SUMMARY RESEARCH SUMMARY **RESEARCH SUMMARY** RESEARCH SUMMARY

Perceptions of a good pupil–teacher relationship

Haydn (2007) collected the views of over 100 teachers, 300 trainees and 700 pupils to identify factors which aid teachers to manage learning effectively. Haydn (2007, pages 115–16) asked pupils which personal characteristics were important in a teacher in order for them to positively influence their attitude to learning. The highest ratings, of 63 per cent, each were a teacher being 'friendly' and a teacher who 'talks to you normally'. Praise and encouragement were rated by 45.7 per cent of the children, compared with a strict approach by 34.8 per cent. In terms of pedagogical characteristics, the most positive traits were of knowing their subject well (78.3 per cent) and being able to explain things well (76.1 per cent). In terms of the behaviour–learning relationship, teachers desired that pupils would listen silently whilst they talked; teachers didn't want to feel restricted as to what activities they could implement because of class management considerations; and they did not want some pupils to hinder the learning of others (Haydn, 2007, page 77).

Children's relationships with you, the trainee

If you are undertaking an ITT course such as a BA or PGCE, which have placements of varying lengths, you are of course limited by time, which has an impact on your ability to develop relationships with the children. Of course, the shorter the placement, the less time you have to build relationships, but the importance of doing so is not lessened.

Upon your first meeting, it is natural for the children to make their own assessments of you, just as you are doing of them. Hayes (2003) suggests that children will be asking themselves a range of questions about you which include whether or not you will be strict, teach interesting lessons, take a personal interest in them, control the naughty children or explain things clearly. He suggests that it is inevitable that children will assume that a trainee is less strict than a qualified teacher unless they prove otherwise. As advised in Chapter 2, ensure that you are calm, firm and authoritative from the outset. This approach will help to set sound foundations for your professional relationship with them.

Trainees often comment on how sad they will be to leave a class. Not matter how short the placement might have been, your presence and your interactions with the children will be influential. Do not underestimate how significant your attention to an individual child may be; how refreshing a new face and a new activity can be for children (irrespective of how effective their teacher is); how empowering for a child it can be if you notice a talent in them that no one else has.

> **REFLECTIVE TASK**
>
> When you are saddened to say goodbye to a class, why is this? Why will you miss them? What did you gain from knowing and teaching these children?

Children's relationships with other staff

While children spend most of their school day with their own teacher and teaching assistants, their relationships with other staff in the school are also important. The word 'staff' refers to all adults working in the school, including the head teacher, other class teachers and TAs, parent helpers, and secretarial, administrative, catering, cleaning and caretaking staff. In each school, the degree of contact they have with children will vary according to factors such as size of the school, its ethos and different approaches from the staff. For example, one head teacher might have a very 'hands on' approach and visit classrooms daily, knowing the children well, while another might remain more office-bound, giving an assembly once a week but not developing strong relationships with the children as individuals. The stronger the relationships are not only between staff and children but also between the staff themselves, the greater the chance of a positive ethos.

For an ethos to be successful – supportive, nurturing and positive – all staff in the school must be involved, not only those with teaching responsibilities. Children are sensitive to the relationships of adults around them and staff tensions can have a negative impact on children's feelings of security. Conversely, when all of the adults are working as a team and have high levels of respect for each other, they serve as positive role models for the children.

For some children, a particular relationship with a member of staff other than their teacher can be particularly rewarding. It is, for example, quite common for a teaching assistant who works closely with a child to form a strong bond. The regular attention derived from a one-to-one, or small group, relationship has the potential to be deeper than that which the teacher can have. By working in small groups, the TA has the potential to get to know the child(ren) well, build their self-esteem and nurture positive behaviour for learning.

Children's relationships with other children

Children need friends. Belonging to communities is an essential part of life, and for children the need to feel a part of a social group, whether large or small, is a significant one. This is recognised in policy, and begins with the EYFS and continues throughout schooling.

CASE STUDY
'You're not my friend anymore'
When Rashid undertook his placement in a Year 5 class, he was amazed by the number of shifts in the friendship groups. *The girls in particular were constantly falling out and some of the behaviour was quite unpleasant. One minute they would be giggling away together, and the next they would be name-calling and vowing never to speak to each other again. An hour later I would see them all back together again laughing as if nothing had ever happened*, he explained.

Fluctuations in social groups are commonplace and natural but can cause distress to children who feel that they have lost their friends, albeit often only temporarily. Such distress is natural as this sense of connectedness, introduced in the previous chapter, is a key part of our spiritual development (Hay and Nye, 2006; Adams *et al.*, 2008). The need to feel that we connect with others in meaningful relationships has a strong bearing on our sense of well-being and is a key ingredient in our social development.

Parents of children and particularly of teenagers are alert to the fact their children's peer groups are highly influential on their behaviour. These influences can be positive or negative, and can impact on a child's manners, motivation to learn, interests and their behaviours in school. You will always need to monitor any potentially damaging forms of peer pressure within your class.

Children's relationships with their family

Children's relationships with their family (parents/carers/siblings/extended family) can have a significant impact upon their behaviour and attitudes towards learning. From birth, the relationship with their parents/carers can have lasting influence. Bowlby (1969) believed that people have an innate desire to be near the people they feel attached to. A baby/young child, when frightened, will feel safe and secure by returning to the person with whom they have formed a strong attachment. When they are separated from that caregiver, they can experience anxiety, as seen when a young child who is sent to a babysitter or to school cries and screams at the parent/carer as they walk away.

Other forms of separation can also have an impact on children's behaviour. Mukherji (2001) details the impact on a child of bereavement, imprisonment of a parent/carer and the more common experience of divorce and separation. With the latter, short-term effects can include defiant and aggressive behaviour and display of negative attitudes. While some families choose not to disclose their personal circumstances to a school, some will do so in order to alert staff to possible changes in behaviour. Jacques (2007) points out that if you are aware of why a child is behaving differently from others or behaving out of character, you are in a stronger position to choose the appropriate strategy to manage it. For example, if you knew that a child's parents were in the process of divorcing, you might react more sympathetically to an aggressive outburst than if you did not know the cause of the behaviour. Naturally, disruption to a child's home life can come at any time and often without warning. A school's good relationships with families are essential, allowing both parties to understand and support the child through difficult times.

A family's approach to raising children can also have a strong bearing on how the child behaves in school, responds to authority figures and how motivated they are to learn.

CASE STUDY
'But my Dad says...'
Simon, an NQT at a large urban primary school in Birmingham, was initially shocked by boys' responses to him when he dealt with a playground fight. Simon was told that a boy who had been hit fought back. When Simon explained the school's policy that a child should walk away and tell a member of staff if they are hit, the child replied *My Dad says that's rubbish. If someone hits you, you have to hit them back, so that's what I did*. Simon had assumed that the school's values would have been shared by all of the parents. This child was not the only one in the school with these views, and the staff had to work hard at conveying their message consistently. They also strived to strengthen relationships with parents/carers so that they were aware of what staff expected from children when on school grounds.

Such conflict between parents' expectations and the school's can raise issues for the children's moral development which you can address as part of SMSC. As Ewens (2007) observes, dilemmas occur with this cross-curricular area. He asks if it is a teacher's job to tell children what is right and what is wrong. If it is, whose moral code should be taught? Or is the job of the teacher to enable children to make their own moral decisions? Whatever you decide is the correct role, disagreements with parents/carers may arise, and it will be important for you to give consistent messages to both children and families in line with your school policy.

In circumstances where children display negative behaviours influenced by home life, it is easy to 'blame the parents'. Visser (2000) warns against this attitude, reminding that many pupils have extreme difficulties to cope with at home, including having an alcoholic or abusive parent, economic hardship or being a carer themselves. Other children might have linguistic or cultural factors which are also impacting upon them. It is thus important that schools build effective relationships with families so that teachers can increase their insight into children's lives. This action will foster understanding and empathy and will avoid the 'blaming' that Visser (2000) discourages. Indeed, as Garner (2005, page 138) observes, recent initiatives on behaviour emphasise a 'no blame' approach which is built on a positive classroom ethos.

Children's relationships with the community

Links with the community are recognised as being an important influence on children. The apparent breakdown in communities over recent decades has concerned many researchers and policy-makers, and one of the government's responses to it has been the Extended Schools initiative. The government aims, by 2010, to give all children access to extended services in schools beyond school hours in its aims to deliver the ECM agenda. These include:

- activities such as music and sport and study support;
- childcare in primary schools;
- support for parents/carers and families;
- easy access to targeted and specialist services;
- community access to facilities.

Extended Schools can improve children's motivation, behaviour and engagement with learning and have a positive impact on raising parental and community aspirations (DCSF, 2007). Lewis (2006) supports the initiative but warns that either caution or a wider understanding of what an extended school might be is necessary. He notes that concerns have been raised over workload for schools, and that there could be potential dangers of institutionalisation for children. Lewis suggests that the extended school needs to be developed along a sustainable ecological framework which moves the idea beyond a school simply being open for longer hours in pursuit of its current agenda with 'wrap-around care' added on.

In the normal course of the timetable, schools can actively participate in building community links. For example, there may be visits to local places of worship in RE, studies of wildlife and landscape for geography or art and visits to care homes for Christmas concerts/PSHCE. A school can also invite different members of the community for a variety of reasons and/or curriculum areas. These include police officers, members of faith communities and local specialists in animal welfare or environmental issues, all of whom can help children to realise that they live in a community and their lives are interdependent with others.

Hughes (2008) advises that there can be many barriers to building links with community, including culture and language. She suggests that schools need to take into account the multicultural nature of such relationships, and need to learn about cultural differences such as different use of body language or different ways of verbal expression.

Yet more relationships

The Behaviour4Learning conceptual framework, as depicted in Chapter 1, also highlighted the influence of relationships with policy and services. Often these are linked, particularly through the ECM agenda which seeks to strengthen multi-agency collaboration. On a day-to-day basis, this agenda can impact on some children through their interaction with external agencies.

PRACTICAL TASK PRACTICAL TASK PRACTICAL TASK PRACTICAL TASK PRACTICAL TASK

Over the course of your placement, note down which professionals visit the school to work with staff and children. Wherever possible, seek the opportunity to talk to them to explore their role further. Remember to fictionalise the names of children in any written records you make.

Professional role of the visitor	Purpose of visits
Educational psychologist	Initial visit to observe Sam's behaviour, as requested by the school and parents. She met with class teacher and mother to detail their concerns and then observed Sam in class. She then talked with Sam privately and made a report, sharing findings with the teacher and parent, and made recommendations for how they could further support Sam.

The influence of relationships on self

The Behaviour4Learning approach recognises that there is an overlap between different types of relationships. An individual's relationship with others influences relationships with self and vice versa. This is exemplified by the effects of peer pressure on children, which can be either positive or negative. For example, if a child seeks to belong to a friendship group who do not value learning, s/he might adopt less on-task behaviour in order to be accepted by the group. In the longer term this action might result in lower achievement and that might impact on self-esteem. Conversely, if children can enjoy an inclusive environment which values and nurtures their spirituality, morality and emotional and social skills, they are likely to develop a strong sense of identity and self-worth which will positively impact on their ability to build positive relationships with others.

A SUMMARY OF **KEY POINTS**

> **Relationships with others are fundamental to aspects of our development.**

> **With a wide range of positive relationships, children are likely to achieve more positive behaviour for learning.**

> **Children's relationships with others have a strong influence on their sense of self.**

MOVING *ON* > > > > > > MOVING *ON* > > > > > > MOVING *ON*

During your induction year, when you are responsible for your own class, you will be able to build stronger relationships with the children, which will also allow you greater insight into their relationships with others, both inside and outside of the school. Theme 1 of the core standards recognises that the learning and development needs of children are best met when teachers develop constructive, respectful relationships with colleagues, learners and their parents or carers. You will thus need to establish fair, trusting, supportive and constructive relationships not only with the children (C1) but also with their parents, carers and colleagues in a collaborative and co-operative way (C4a, C4b, C4c, C41). By promoting children's self-control, independence and co-operation via the development of their social, emotional and behavioural skills (C39), you can help them to build stronger relationships with others.

FURTHER READING FURTHER READING **FURTHER READING** FURTHER READING

Lewis, B (2005) *What do you stand for? For kids – a guide to building character.* Minneapolis: Free Spirit Publishing. This book offers practical activities to help children develop a sense of identity and build relationships with others. It is written for children to read. Although aimed at an American audience, strong readers will be able to navigate through the American phrases and spellings such as 'kids', 'neighbors' and 'fourth grade'.

Mortimer, H (2008) *All about me: exciting play activities that support the Early Years Foundation Stage.* Haddenham: Folens Publishers. This book provides practical play-based activities for all Early Years teachers. The games' foci include family, friends, feelings and time alone.

Weare, K (2004) *Developing the emotionally literate school.* London: Paul Chapman. Weare offers a detailed and accessible account of the concept of emotional literacy, together with practical suggestions for how schools can develop their school according to its principles.

REFERENCES REFERENCES **REFERENCES** REFERENCES **REFERENCES** REFERENCES

Adams, K, Hyde, B and Woolley, R (2008) *The spiritual dimension of childhood.* London: Jessica Kingsley

Bowlby, J (1969) *Child care and growth of love.* London: Penguin

DCSF (2007) *Extended schools: building on experience.* Nottingham: DCSF. Available from: www.teachernet.gov.uk/publications, accessed 2 August 2008

DCSF (2008) *Early Years Foundation Stage.* Nottingham: HMSO

Ewens, T (2007) Spiritual, moral, social and cultural values in the classroom, in K Jacques and R Hyland (eds) *Professional studies: primary and early years.* Exeter: Learning Matters

Gardner, H (1983) *Frames of mind: the theory of multiple intelligences.* New York: Basic Books

Garner, P (2005) Behaviour for learning: a positive approach to managing classroom behaviour, in S Capel, M Leask and T Turner (eds) *Learning to teach in the secondary school: a companion to school experience.* Abingdon: Routlege

Goleman, D (2004) *Emotional intelligence and working with emotional intelligence (omnibus).* London: Bloomsbury

Hay, D and Nye, R (2006) *The spirit of the child.* London: Jessica Kingsley

Haydn, T (2007) *Managing pupil behaviour: key issues in teaching and learning.* Abingdon: Routledge

Hayes, D (2003) *A student teacher's guide to primary school placement: learning to survive and prosper.* London: Routledge

Hughes, P (2008) *Principles of primary education study guide.* London: David Fulton

Jacques, K (2007) Managing challenging behaviour, in K Jacques and R Hyland (eds) *Professional studies: primary and early years.* Exeter: Learning Matters

Lewis, J (2006) The school's role in encouraging behaviour for learning outside the classroom that supports learning within. A response to the 'Every Child Matters' and Extended Schools initiatives. *Support for Learning*, 21 (4), 175–81

Mukherji, P (2001) *Understanding children's challenging behaviour.* Cheltenham: Nelson Thornes

Rogers, C (1983) *Freedom to learn for the 80s.* Columbus: Charles E. Merrill

Salovey, P and Mayer, J D (1990) Emotional intelligence. *Imagination, Cognition and Personality*, 9: 3

Visser, J (2000) *Managing behaviour in classrooms.* London: David Fulton

Weare, K (2004) *Developing the emotionally literate school.* London: Paul Chapman

5
In the classroom: children's relationships with the curriculum

Chapter objectives

By the end of this chapter you should be able to:

- **reflect on the implications of policy on children's relationships to the curriculum;**
- **understand the importance of teachers' and children's relationships to the curriculum in behaviour for learning;**
- **explore key influences affecting children's relationships to the curriculum, and attitudes towards learning.**

This chapter addresses the following Professional Standards for QTS:

Q3a, Q3b, Q10, Q14, Q15, Q18, Q19, Q20, Q22, Q25a, Q25b, Q25c, Q25d, Q30

Links to: Early Years Foundation Stage (EYFS); all curriculum subjects; spiritual, moral, social and cultural development (SMSC); personal, social and health and citizenship education (PSHCE); Every Child Matters (ECM); personalised learning.

Introduction

Given that learning and behaviour are inextricably linked, it is necessary to focus on children's relationship with the curriculum. The EPPI report (2004) emphasises that teachers who promote children's progress in learning in a meaningful curriculum will be at an advantage in creating a positive behavioural environment. In an ideal world, teachers would all be highly effective in delivering an inspiring curriculum and all children would be fully engaged in learning. However, even the most motivated child who has a strong identity and high self-esteem will have different responses to different components of their timetable.

> ## CASE STUDY
> **Making Music**
> Colin attended the parents' evening of his 11-year-old son, Aaron. The class teacher explained that Aaron worked conscientiously in all lessons, showing interest and an eagerness to learn. However, in music – which was taken by a visiting music specialist – he was 'almost a different child.' He would regularly disobey the teacher, play around with the instruments, make inappropriate noises in singing sessions and distract other children. When Colin asked Aaron why his behaviour was different in music he explained that he disliked the visiting teacher, finding her too strict and not paying him any attention. In addition, he found it difficult to keep a beat when playing instruments and he felt that the teacher was impatient with him even though *it wasn't his fault he couldn't do it*.

It is natural for children to be more highly motivated and conscientious in some curriculum areas than others. The situation is no different for adults such as yourself who are undertaking further study, or for primary teachers who have to teach a wide range of subjects. It is not always simply a case of either liking or disliking a subject that affects our behaviour for learning. In Aaron's case, for example, the dynamics of his relationship with the music teacher (or at least his perception of them) were a key factor, in addition to his perceived difficulties in the subject. Take a few moments to consider your own responses, both conscious and subconscious, to various components of your own curriculum in further or higher education.

REFLECTIVE TASK

Reflect on your attitude towards different lectures on your current or previous course. What made you excited about certain sessions? Why were you less interested in learning in others? Consider the influence of: the effectiveness of the tutor; the effectiveness of the teaching strategies; your like or dislike of the subject; how relevant you thought the content was; how well you progressed in the subject.

If you have analysed why you are positive about participating in certain sessions, also think about your behaviour for learning. It is likely that you also portray appropriate behaviour for learning. As discussed in Chapter 1, you might display several of the following characteristics: engagement, collaboration, participation, communication, motivation, independent activity, responsiveness, self-regard, self-esteem and responsibility. These are the characteristics that you would hope to witness in all of your pupils, but achieving this involves understanding a range of factors.

This chapter explores those factors which enable learners to engage with a curriculum in positive ways. It begins with a discussion about policy and how it can affect the teacher's role in facilitating children's positive relationships with the curriculum. The chapter then focuses on how teachers can facilitate children's positive relationship with the curriculum and considers some potential difficulties with regard to that task.

Curriculum policy

The curriculum you encounter when you enter schools is regularly developing. In 1988 the National Curriculum was implemented and it has undergone considerable revisions since then, as outlined below. The curriculum is designed to be relevant to children, and is accompanied by the expectation that children will enjoy their learning, as the *Excellence and enjoyment* (DfES, 2003) document conveys. Its delivery requires a range of skills which overlap, and a sound understanding of pedagogy as detailed in Chapter 2.

The impact of policy on relationships with the curriculum

In addition to skilful delivery, there are also further challenges facing teachers which can inhibit the development of positive relationships with the curriculum for both teachers and children. Here, some of these changes and challenges are considered.

The content of the curriculum has undergone numerous changes since 1988. These changes include the implementation of the National Literacy Strategy (1998) and the National

Numeracy Strategy (1999) which altered curriculum content and also introduced new teaching methods. As you are aware, more recently, the Primary National Strategy has focused on raising standards, combined with 'making learning fun'. The *goal for every primary school [is] to combine excellence in teaching with enjoyment of learning* (DfES, 2003, page 4). The government goes on to describe what is observed in outstanding schools, where children are engaged by learning which stretches them and also *excites their imagination. They enjoy the richness of their learning* (DfES, 2003, page 9). A variety of teaching strategies is essential, and learning takes place not only in the classroom but also outside, and with people other than their class teacher, including parents and grandparents, occurring in formal and informal ways. The document calls for each school to develop its own distinct identity and to develop its own rich and varied curricula.

Naturally, all changes to the curriculum are brought in with the best intentions. They are aimed to improve the education which children receive, and to ensure that all children learn and develop to their full potential. Reflective practice, which is essential to educators, inevitably brings changes to policy as each component is reviewed, refined and developed, and research is undertaken to further inform that policy. A major example of continuing change is the Primary Review – an independent enquiry into primary education in England. It is based at the University of Cambridge and supported by the Esmée Fairbairn Foundation. It is the largest comprehensive investigation of English primary education since the Plowden enquiry of 1967 and its remit includes exploration of the purposes and values of primary education, the curriculum and learning environment, the adequacy of current provision and the findings of national and international research. Its funding ends in late 2008, and its final report is due to be published shortly after. You can keep updated by consulting the Primary Review's website (www.primaryreview.org.uk).

Teachers' relationships with the curriculum

The regular changes in the curriculum witnessed over the past 20 years have had a major impact on teachers. As with all changes and initiatives, opinion will differ among people affected.

CASE STUDY

Curriculum changes – for better or worse?

Jasmine, a teacher, welcomed the National Curriculum because she believed it brought a much needed continuity for the country. She had been worried that some of her colleagues had been neglecting important aspects of the humanities because they simply did not value them or see their importance in a child's life. Without strong leadership in their school, some teachers had been able to provide a limited curriculum. Another colleague, who had always been committed to providing a holistic curriculum, felt that the idea of the National Curriculum was admirable but was anxious that it was too prescriptive, and limited teachers' professionalism in being able to mould the curriculum they taught.

As a student about to enter the teaching profession in the twenty-first century, you will undoubtedly see many more changes to the curriculum and to other aspects of your professional life as educational reforms continue.

REFLECTIVE TASK

Can you identify areas of the curriculum which you think need to be changed? Have you met professionals with different views? How do you think you will respond to regular changes in your professional life?

Shortly after the Literacy and Numeracy Strategies were introduced, studies highlighted that the restructuring of the education system in the years immediately following the launch of the National Curriculum was a major source of stress for teachers. Troman and Woods (2001) found that the demands on teachers to provide paperwork for Ofsted as evidence of their professionalism was a source of high workload and subsequent stress. At the same time, Smithers and Robinson (2001) highlighted the low retention rates of teachers and interviewed those who were leaving the profession. Amongst the primary teachers, 73.9 per cent referred to the workload and 42.1 per cent to government initiatives as reasons for leaving (Smithers and Robinson, 2001; Adams, 2002). For many teachers, restructuring of the curriculum and related government policies have been a continued source of stress, and concerns over teacher retention continue.

Current policy: a paradox?

Policy always has its critics and Turner-Bisset (2007) draws attention to what she sees as a potential paradox in educational thinking with regard to the current curriculum which emphasises creativity and enjoyment. She describes how policy has become focused on a performative discourse, i.e. being based around learning objectives, evidence, efficiency, accountability as measured by Ofsted and Standard Assessment Tests (SATS) results. At the same time, the Primary National Strategy has emphasised the enjoyment aspect of learning and has offered schools the opportunity to make their own decisions about how long to spend on each subject and has encouraged them to take control of their curriculum and be innovative. Turner-Bisset (2007) argues that schools will be reluctant to do so given that testing remains in place, and points to Ofsted's (2005) observation that most schools have concentrated on raising standards but have been more cautious about taking a flexible approach to their curriculum.

REFLECTIVE TASK

How far do you think it is possible to deliver an exciting curriculum? Do national tests and league tables restrict teachers making innovative changes to their curriculum?

Teachers and trainees need to develop positive relationships with a curriculum in order to facilitate children doing the same. Where staff are feeling negative, these attitudes will be conveyed through teaching (albeit subconsciously) and children's learning may suffer. You will need to strengthen your relationship with those curriculum areas you feel less competent in, or feel are less important than others, to ensure that you consistently offer children the highest standard of teaching across the timetable.

Children's relationships with the curriculum

For some children, the ability to form relationships with the curriculum is hindered by additional factors such as learning or emotional and behavioural difficulties. These difficulties warrant a more in-depth focus, and are thus dealt with separately in the following chapter. For now, the focus is on some key factors which can affect children's relationships with different areas of the curriculum.

A primary teacher has the particularly challenging task of having to deliver a wide range of subjects. These subjects of course have particular features which lend themselves to different teaching methods. PE is inherently practical and active for example, and does not demand the reading skills required in other subjects such as literacy. That said, all subjects benefit from a diversity of teaching strategies in order to give children variation and meet their different learning needs. One way forward is to bring increased creativity into the curriculum – a move supported by a range of professional organisations in education, as well as the government.

Creativity in the curriculum

The notion of encouraging creativity in the curriculum has recently gathered momentum but is not new. Brundrett (2007) notes that primary education in the 1950s, 1960s and 1970s saw a move away from a Victorian tradition of 'chalk and talk' to a new vision characterised by creative learning. New buildings were designed, displays of children's work became commonplace, children entered a world of learning by experience and new teaching styles dominated classrooms. In recent times, however, since the introduction of the National Curriculum, Ofsted inspections and evidence-based testing, there has been a quest to bring more creativity back into lessons.

The National Advisory Committee on Creative and Cultural Education (NACCCE), was established in 1998 to make recommendations to the government on the creative and cultural development of young people in both formal and informal educational settings. In 1999 it published its report, entitled *All our futures: creativity culture and education*, which has remained influential. They argued that creativity should be developed through all curriculum areas – an argument which has since been echoed by other organisations and researchers (NACCCE, 1999). For example, The National College for School Leadership (NCSL) states that creativity for learning is not simply about giving the arts and humanities more time on the curriculum. Rather it focuses on developing pupils' creative thinking and behaviour through a rich curriculum (NCSL, 2004).

NACCCE (1999) defined creativity as *imaginative activity fashioned so as to produce outcomes that are both original and of value*. Creative processes, the report suggests, have four key characteristics.

- They involve thinking or behaving in an imaginative way.
- The imaginative element is purposeful and is aimed towards an objective.
- The processes result in something which is original.
- The outcome must be of value in relation to the objective.

However, NACCCE emphasises the importance of each school developing its own understanding of creativity in order to build a shared understanding as a foundation for their work in this area.

Creativity is promoted in the Primary National Strategy (DFES, 2003) and QCA have provided materials called *Creativity: find it, promote it*, which are available online, and offer practical suggestions for teachers and head teachers. The Statutory Framework for the Early Years Foundation Stage (DCSF, 2008) also highlights children's creative development, including it as one of the six areas covered by the Early Learning Goals and educational programmes. It states that their creativity must be extended by supporting their curiosity, exploration and play. What conditions are required for promoting children's creativity in the classroom?

Conditions for creativity in the classroom

NACCCE (1999) suggests that pupils need the space to express their own ideas and feelings, and must be given the freedom to experiment – supported by the necessary skills and understanding. Teachers need to provide the time for creativity to develop, because if critical appraisal is applied too early to a project, then enthusiasm for it can be highly demotivated. Pupils should be encouraged to use their imagination and to be original – they should express their curiosity and question. Ofsted (2003), using NACCCE's definition of creativity outlined above, identifies conditions which best enable pupils to be creative. Where best practice is observed, teachers and senior management are committed to its promotion. Teachers have a clear understanding of what it means to be creative and also possess a range of sound pedagogical skills which they apply to ensure that creativity is developed in all pupils irrespective of their ability. Children are given the freedom to think 'outside the box' and are given opportunities for learning in which there is no clear solution.

QCA emphasises that tasks should be personally and culturally authentic and where possible should build on children's interests and experiences, and be incorporated into current planning. Experimentation, problem-solving, discussion and collaboration all have the potential to provide opportunities for creative thinking and behaviour. In the Early Years, teachers should provide young children with the opportunities to explore and share their thoughts, ideas and feelings through a variety of different activities (DCSF, 2008).

Creativity and behaviour

Why is creativity important when considering children's behaviour for learning? As you have seen, learning and behaviour are closely linked and as the Primary National Strategy observes, creativity is a powerful means of engaging children with their learning. When teachers plan for and respond to children's creative ideas, the children become increasingly curious to discover new things (DfES, 2003).

In a project commissioned by the National Teacher Research Panel in 2004, two partnership primary schools were studied in order to gain further insight into the development of a creative culture in schools. One of the outcomes of the project was that teachers reported a reduction in disaffected children. By providing a more creative curriculum which was based on a shared vision and philosophy, learning became more enriching and exciting for both teachers and children. In interviews, the children commented that their learning skills felt more relevant (Casserley, 2004).

Earlier, in Chapter 3, you saw how a child's self-esteem and motivation are fundamental influences on their behaviour for learning. QCA, on their website, argues that creativity improves pupils' self-esteem and motivation, as well as their levels of achievement. This occurs because children become more interested in making new discoveries independently, are open to new ideas and eager to work collaboratively to explore them. They are keen to work beyond formal lessons to pursue their ideas (http://curriculum.qca.org.uk).

> ### CASE STUDY
> **I can do it!**
>
> Alex was a seven-year-old boy who suffered from low self-esteem in most areas of learning. He struggled with most subjects, partly because of his low reading age, which impacted on him throughout much of the curriculum. Alex's new teacher believed that creativity was important and she implemented more opportunities for creativity than her predecessors had done. Characteristic of her methods were group discussion tasks and practical activities which were open-ended. Alex thrived in this new environment and began to demonstrate high levels of enthusiasm and frequently made valuable verbal contributions to the group. After completing a 3D group display in science, he was overheard telling a friend, *I love science now – I can do it!* His teacher observed in Alex increased self-esteem and motivation, as well as higher levels of initiative and independence, in many subjects over the course of the year.

As with all theory and policy, there are critics, and the notion of creativity in the curriculum is no exception. Turner-Bisset (2007) critiques the definition offered by NACCCE and the material on the QCA website. She poses the question of whether or not creative activity needs to be purposeful all the time, and is concerned that such an implication relates to the emphasis on performance and evidence-based results. She also raises the issue of value – if creativity is to be valued, then who is it to be valued by? You can explore her ideas further and form your own opinions.

The range of curriculum subjects

The number and diversity of curriculum subjects that are taught in a primary school, together with SMSC and PSHCE, can present significant challenges for teachers in their quest to enable all children to engage positively with all areas of the curriculum. It is natural that each of us, adult and child alike, has preferences for different subjects and has differing skills and interests. For example, some prefer more logical, rational-oriented studies such as maths and science, and others feel more comfortable with creating artwork or poetry. While it is too simplistic to assume that children who enjoy maths will not like poetry, one of your challenges in the classroom is to know the individual children's preferences well so that you can increase motivation for learning in the subjects which children are less enthusiastic about. Consider your role in delivering the primary curriculum by looking at the list of subjects you need to cover (PSHCE and modern foreign languages are non-statutory and the latter relates to Key Stage 2) as outlined in Figure 5.1.

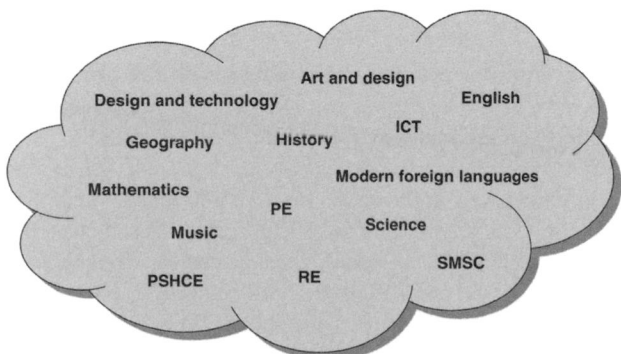

Figure 5.1 Key Stage 1 and Key Stage 2 curricula

How do you feel about tackling all of these areas? You will need to reflect carefully on your attitude towards them because your relationship with the curriculum is important too. You need to take an objective look at your attitudes towards the curriculum areas because it is possible that you are conveying, albeit unconsciously, less interest in some of them. Hood (2008) undertook a small-scale study in one Year 4 class of 31 pupils to explore their perceptions of learning. Nearly all of the children said that they liked the majority of subjects but when asked which subject they most disliked, 72 per cent reported either geography or RE, and none of the remaining 28 per cent ranked them as their favourite subject. For this class, the finding is significant and serves as a good example for further exploration. Hood (2008) suggests that because the children had the same teacher for all subjects, teacher personality was not an issue in determining these dislikes. However, many other factors affect children's response to a subject. Could it be that the teacher was not as enthusiastic about geography or RE as s/he was about other curriculum areas and this was reflected in how s/he conveyed them? Hood (2008) continues to say that the class as a whole appeared to prefer practical work and favoured subjects such as art and design and technology. Geography and RE offer many opportunities for practical work too – could it be that the teacher did not utilise those opportunities?

PRACTICAL TASK PRACTICAL TASK PRACTICAL TASK PRACTICAL TASK PRACTICAL TASK

Your curriculum preferences

Put the curriculum subjects in order of preference and note down the reasons for the order you have placed them. Two examples are given for you.

Subjects	Favourite	Reasons
History		It has always been my passion. It's vital for children to know so they can gain a sense of their place in the world...
PE	↓	PE is so difficult to teach because behaviour management is always difficult. I was never chosen for teams when I was a child
	Least favourite	

So, how can you develop more positive relationships with the areas which are your least favourite? Of course, one of the key ways forward is to develop a range of teaching strategies which inspire and engage children in learning. You will need to investigate examples of excellent teaching in those fields to gather new approaches, for example. However, by reflecting on why you have a less enthusiastic response to some areas than others, you can recognise why you respond as you do and seek appropriate new tactics. If, as in the practical task above, you dislike teaching PE because you were never chosen for teams when you were at primary school, then you can ensure that the children in your care do not encounter the same treatment. You can do this by pre-arranging teams which have a combination of lower and higher sporting abilities. If you are having difficulties with behaviour in PE, you can investigate strategies which are particularly relevant to PE and to children moving around in order to develop your practice.

Identity and relationship with the curriculum

In Chapter 3 you learnt how a child's sense of self has many interrelated components which include self-efficacy, self-esteem, self-confidence and motivation. These aspects of self also have a strong bearing on relationship with curriculum. Further, other factors can also be influential.

CASE STUDY
A budding architect

Charlotte was a Year 6 pupil who had always shown a talent for drawing. Her pictorial work was characterised by intricate detail and creativity – not only could she copy well but she could also produce original drawings. Since she was very young she had had a fascination for buildings and this was represented in her work. Her parents regularly told teachers how Charlotte would eventually train as an architect.

For Charlotte, part of her identity was as a future architect. This ambition was further influenced and reinforced by her parents, and her teachers particularly encouraged her work in art and design and design and technology. Charlotte had high levels of self-efficacy in these subjects and also had high levels of motivation. In the view of her teachers, Charlotte had a positive relationship with these curriculum areas.

Relationships outside of school can also have a strong negative impact on a child's response to the curriculum. Children who come from homes where education is not valued might show little interest in their lessons – they might not 'see the point' in learning about numbers, how to read maps or why magnets attract some materials and not others. Such children pose a strong challenge to teachers, and excellent teaching and strong relationships will be highly important to engage and motivate children at least for part of the time.

Self-efficacy, self-esteem, self-confidence and motivation

Nurturing children's self-efficacy, esteem, confidence and motivation are long-term affairs. Children need to feel that they are being treated as individuals and feel that they are 'known' – not simply an anonymous face in a large crowd. To develop these aspects of self in relation to the curriculum, personalised learning is a means of doing so. In schools, the term relates to tailoring education to individual needs, interests and aptitudes. The DfES (2004) identifies five key components.

- **Assessment for learning.** Through AfL, teachers offer clear feedback to children on what they do best and how they can improve their work. This dialogue is evidence-based and identifies every child's learning needs.
- **Effective teaching and learning strategies.** These require a range of whole-class, group and individual methods which engage and stretch children.
- **Curriculum entitlement and choice.** Primary teachers are encouraged to bring flexibility and creativity into their curriculum, as outlined above.

- **School organisation.** Teachers and senior management are asked to think creatively about the organisation of their school.
- **Strong partnership beyond school.** It is essential that parents and carers are involved in their children's learning, and initiatives to make those relationships stronger are encouraged.

These principles for personalised learning have very clear links with the B4L approach: they seek to increase children's engagement with the curriculum by making it more relevant, personal and creative. They are inclusive because they cater for all children and also take account of the need for children's relationships with others.

This chapter has highlighted the importance for children and teachers to maintain good relationships with the curriculum. It has not been able to offer simple answers because there are many interrelated factors which influence our attitudes towards the curriculum. However, some practical advice is offered in Chapter 7.

A SUMMARY OF **KEY POINTS**

> **Policy on curriculum development has a range of implications not only for children's relationships with the curriculum but also for teachers' relationships with it.**

> **Your relationship with the curriculum is important.**

> **The delivery of a motivating and inspiring curriculum will empower children to develop positive relationships with it.**

MOVING *ON* > > > > > > MOVING *ON* > > > > > > MOVING *ON*

To enable children to strengthen their relationships with the curriculum, you will need to ensure that you develop your professional knowledge of pedagogy by having an up-to-date knowledge of teaching and learning strategies (C10) and of curriculum areas and cross-curricular learning (C15). In order to offer personalised learning (C19) you will also need to know assessment requirements, approaches to assessment and offer constructive feedback on children's learning so that they can develop further (C11, C12, C14, C32). Your careful planning, which takes account of assessment, can enable you to set appropriate learning objectives which allow children to consolidate and extend their learning (C26, C27, C28, C31). Through encouraging children to reflect on their learning, they will be able to develop a sense of ownership (C33, C36).

The next chapter focuses upon additional factors which can potentially complicate children's development of relationships with self, others and curriculum, particularly learning and emotional and behavioural difficulties.

FURTHER READING FURTHER READING FURTHER READING FURTHER READING

DFES (2003) *Excellence and enjoyment – a strategy for primary schools.* London: DFES. This document lays out the aims for the Primary National Strategy. You can download it from the DCSF website (www.standards.dcsf.gov.uk).

QCA *Creativity: find it, promote it.* These materials offer practical advice for teachers and head teachers on promoting creativity in schools. Case studies are provided to exemplify points. (They are available via: www.ncaction.org.uk and http://curriculum.qca.org.uk).

The Primary Review...children, their world, their education (2008). This website offers the latest information on the review of England's primary education system. It has sections for teachers, children and parents and useful downloads. (You can access their website at http://www.primary review.org.uk).

REFERENCES REFERENCES **REFERENCES** REFERENCES **REFERENCES** REFERENCES

Adams, K (2002) Losing control: the effects of educational restructuring on waking and dream life. *International Journal of Children's Spirituality*, 7(2): 183–92

Brundrett, M (2007) Bringing creativity back into primary education. *Education 3–13*, 35(2): 105–7

Casserley (2004) *Developing a creative culture*. National Teacher Research Panel. Available from: www.standards.dfes.gov.uk/ntrp/publications/Casserley/, accessed 20 October 2008

DCSF (2008) *Early Years Foundation Stage.* Nottingham: HMSO

DfES (2003) *Excellence and enjoyment – a strategy for primary schools.* London: DfES

DfES (2004) *A national conversation about personalised learning.* Nottingham: DfES

EPPI (2004) *A systematic review of how theories explain learning behaviour in school contexts.* Available from: www.behaviour4learning.ac.uk, accessed 7 January 2008

Hood, P (2008) What do we teachers need to know to enhance our creativity? A report on a pilot project into primary school pupils' perceptions of their identities as learners. *Education 3–13*, 36(2): 139–51

National Advisory Committee on Creative and Cultural Education (NACCCE) (1999) *All our futures: creativity culture and education.* Sudbury: DfEE

National College for School Leadership (NCSL 2004). Available at: www.ncsl.org.uk/, accessed 5 July 2008

Ofsted (2003) *Expect the Unexpected: developing creativity in primary and secondary schools.* An E-publication, available from www.ofsted.gov.uk/assets/3377.pdf, accessed 10 August 2008

Ofsted (2005) *Primary National Strategy: an evaluation of its impact in primary schools 2004/05.* Available at: www.ofsted.gov.uk/Publications-and-research/Education/Providers/Primary-schools/Primary-National-Strategy-an-evaluation-of-its-impact-in-primary-schools-2004-05/(language)eng-GB accessed 20 October 2008

Ofsted (2007) *The annual report of her majesty's chief inspector of education, children's services and skills 2006/2007.* London: The Stationery Office

Smithers, A and Robinson, P (2001) *Teachers leaving.* London: NUT

Troman, G and Woods, P (2001) *Primary teachers' stress.* London: Routledge Falmer

Turner-Bisset, R (2007) Performativity by stealth: a critique of recent initiatives on creativity. *Education 3–13*, 35(2): 193–203

6
Additional factors

Chapter objectives

By the end of this chapter you should be able to:

- **understand the additional factors which can further complicate relationships with self, others and curriculum;**
- **acknowledge the complexities of the theories of relationships with self, others and curriculum;**
- **know the procedures for seeking assistance with children who have special educational needs.**

This chapter addresses the following Professional Standards for QTS:

Q3a, Q4, Q18, Q19, Q20, Q21a, Q21b

Links to: Every Child Matters (ECM); child and adolescent mental health services (CAMHS); special educational needs (SEN); inclusive education.

Introduction

You will be fully aware from your own relationships with self and others, whether they are with siblings, parents, friends, colleagues or partners, that relationships are complicated. Critical comments from others can damage your self-esteem and have a negative impact on your relationship with self. Sometimes people act in unexpected ways, which changes your understanding of the relationship. Setbacks on your training course can damage your previously positive response to it.

The advice offered throughout this book on the importance of relationships and how to nurture them cannot solve all of the challenges you will encounter because of the complexity of human interactions and the wide range of influences upon them, some of which you will have no control over. Further, some children in your class will have additional factors which affect their behaviour for learning, which take the form of special educational needs (SEN).

In Chapter 1 you saw that the government's policy on inclusion seeks to give all children a full education within mainstream schools. This policy means that it is inevitable that, over the course of your placements and beyond, you will have children in your class who have some form of SEN whether it be a learning difficulty, a physical disability, a social, emotional and behavioural difficulty and/or mental health issues. This chapter cannot detail the causes and characteristics of all special needs, but instead explores a selection of frequently occurring ones to highlight how they can impinge on a child's relationships with self, others and/or curriculum. (The inclusion of specific disorders and difficulties does not imply that they are any more significant than those which have not been detailed and you should refer to specialised literature for more information on all the different needs.) After a consideration of some types of special educational needs and the influence they can have on behaviour for learning, the chapter then shows you how to seek support when working with children with SEN.

Learning difficulties

There is a wide range of recognised conditions which are associated with the term 'learning difficulties', although debate and controversy exist over the diagnosis, treatment and prevalence of some. In several cases there can be an overlap of learning difficulties and social, emotional and behavioural difficulties and you will need to read this chapter with that overlap in mind.

Dyslexia

There is considerable debate over the definition of dyslexia, but it is generally considered to be the most common type of specific learning disability (others include dyscalculia and dyspraxia). In general terms, dyslexia is a potentially severe reading disability which is not related to low cognitive ability and can manifest in failure to recognise high-frequency words, the reversal of letters when writing, and phonetic spelling which is incorrect (Ayers, 2006).

Lack of diagnosis is particularly common with dyslexia. O'Flynn *et al.* (2003) note that dyslexic children are often incorrectly labelled as inattentive, lazy or poorly motivated. They argue that it is one of the most debilitating conditions emotionally and socially because it is so prone to escaping detection. The potential impact of learning disabilities like dyslexia, dyscalculia and dyspraxia on behaviour for learning are complex and each case is different. However, there is always the potential for a child to become frustrated if the curriculum is not fully accessible to them, which can lead to low-level disruption such as avoidance tactics or to more aggressive outbursts which stem from that frustration. The relationship with self can also be hindered because low attainment or feelings of 'difference' can dent self-esteem and self-confidence.

Autistic spectrum disorders

The term 'autistic spectrum disorders' refers to a wide and varied range of characteristics of autism which occur along a continuum. Children with autism tend to show impairments in social interaction, often lacking interest in friendships and not being able to empathise. Communication issues can also occur in the form of delayed language development or repetition of what has been heard. Autistic children usually need very repetitive routines and any disruption to it can lead to outbursts of negative behaviour. Ayers (2006) states that only 20 per cent of children with autism have IQs in the normal range, with 75 per cent having IQs below 70. However, Jones (2002) notes that it is difficult to gather statistics on children with autistic spectrum disorders who have learning difficulties.

Children with Asperger's syndrome are thought to have a higher functioning form of autism (Ayers, 2006) although some researchers believe that it is a different form of disability (Westwood, 2006). Asperger's includes the social and behavioural elements of autism but not the cognitive and language deficits. Older children tend to have a narrow range of interests and might focus on memorising lists or have advanced musical or artistic skills (Ayers, 2006). Jones (2002) adds that children may also have different sensory perception and responses to others which can manifest as over- or under-sensitivity in comparison with their peers.

As Jones (2002) points out, the variety of forms of autism means that there is no single type of intervention possible. Children who are on the autistic spectrum will experience some difficulties in learning via traditional teaching methods. While some attend special units, run either by the local authority or by independent organisations, other children will be placed in mainstream schools. The mainstream teacher will need to make provision for the child's needs because the child cannot be expected to fit into the school's existing routines and structures. It will thus be essential that the child's views are sought because distress and conflict can occur if the child cannot cope with the existing regime (Jones, 2002).

Social, emotional and behavioural difficulties, and mental health

As noted in Chapter 1, children with social, emotional and behavioural difficulties (SEBD) present a significant challenge to schools becoming inclusive settings. The fear of many teachers and parents is the potential threat to other members of the school (Rooney, 2002). It is particularly important over the course of your training and induction that you begin to develop a full understanding of the types of SEBD that occur, and the action you and your colleagues can take to help the children involved.

The DfEE's (2001) guidance on children's mental health suggests that those with social, emotional and behavioural problems which are outside the normal range for their age or gender can also be described as experiencing mental health problems or disorders. However, the report goes on to emphasise that the term SEBD is one that is usually related to an educational context whereas mental health terminology is used by medical practitioners. Thus a child who exhibits challenging behaviour in school might be classified as having SEBD in the educational context but might be described as having a conduct disorder in the medical context. The DfEE document stresses that not all children with mental health problems will necessarily have special educational needs.

There is growing awareness and understanding of mental health issues which affect some children, as well as adults. Research shows an increase in the number of children experiencing mental health problems, with an estimate of 10 per cent of children aged between 5 and 15 in this category (DfEE, 2001).

ADD and ADHD

One group of the more common problems which some children face is hyperkinetic disorders, which include the disturbance of activity and attention (DfEE, 2001). Attention deficit disorder and attention deficit hyperactivity disorder – known more commonly as ADD and ADHD respectively – are examples. These are conditions where children have severe difficulties in maintaining attention, concentration or controlling motor activity. Such children are usually restless, talkative and easily distracted (Ayers, 2006; Westwood, 2006). There is no single test or checklist for diagnosis, and controversy exists over the conditions. Westwood (2006) suggests that children can be inappropriately labelled with ADD and ADHD when they are simply bored or restless. Further, some medics deny that the conditions even exist.

Children who exhibit the characteristic behaviours of ADD and ADHD are likely to struggle to form relationships with others and with the curriculum. Classmates may find their lack of concentration frustrating and seek to avoid friendships with them, which in turn can impact on their relationship with self if they do not feel connected to others. Their behaviour can distract learning for those around them as well as for themselves. Westwood (2006) observes that while these children are not necessarily below average in intelligence, their inability to focus on tasks means that their achievement is often poor. This has considerable implications for the teacher, who may need to adapt their teaching to suit the children's needs. This may include providing strong visual inputs, using computer-assisted learning and teaching the children self-management skills.

Other mental health issues

The DfEE (2001, page 1) guidelines on mental health list other issues which are reported in children. These include:

- emotional disorders such as phobias, anxiety and depression;
- conduct disorders including stealing, defiance and aggression;
- attachment disorders;
- developmental disorders;
- eating disorders;
- habit disorders such as soiling or sleeping problems;
- post-traumatic stress syndromes;
- somatic disorders such as chronic fatigue syndrome;
- psychotic disorders including schizophrenia and manic depression.

While children with mental health issues such as these will be in the minority, their situations will be extremely distressing for the children, their families and all who engage with them. Specialist help will be essential and is available through inter-agency collaboration.

Child and adolescent mental health services (CAMHS) is a term used to embrace all services which contribute in some way to the mental health care of children and young people, such as those provided by health, education, social services or other agencies. The term CAMHS is also used more narrowly to refer to specialist mental health services which might include clinical psychologists, child psychotherapists or music therapists. CAMHS is thus a multi-agency operation, working in line with the ECM agenda. Although not a rigid structure, there are four tiers which are used as a conceptual framework, with tier four being the level at which children with the most serious problems are seen. At this tier, eating disorder units or specialist teams for children who have been abused might be involved. You can learn more about how CAMHS operates on the Every Child Matters website (see useful websites, below).

PRACTICAL TASK PRACTICAL TASK PRACTICAL TASK PRACTICAL TASK PRACTICAL TASK

As you move through your placements, make notes on children who have different learning difficulties, SEBD and mental health issues. Observe how these can impact on the children's behaviour for learning and make notes on how staff support these children.

Other issues

The increased awareness of special educational needs has been invaluable for children, families and professionals alike. Nevertheless, many challenges still remain. For you as a trainee, there are other issues which may be of immediate concern. Birkett (2007) distinguishes between troublesome and troubled children and emphasises that teachers should understand the difference between the two. The former create problems in the classroom through choice, while the latter's behaviour is a consequence of trauma, such as abuse, and requires specialist help from external agencies. Further, conditions such as ADD, ADHD or autistic spectrum disorders can be causes of troubled behaviour but so too can depression, anxiety or obsessive compulsive disorders.

Further, you may also teach children who have physical disabilities. While these disabilities are not linked to behavioural problems, on occasions they can lead to disruptive behaviour due to frustrations which you will need to minimise. Instances include a visually impaired child who may become irritated if they cannot fully access teaching materials, and a child in a wheelchair who may become momentarily irritated if they cannot manoeuvre through a corridor which is partially blocked.

Procedures for identifying and managing SEN

All children who have learning difficulties are especially vulnerable to not developing affirming relationships with self and curriculum. These two components can interact with each other – when a child struggles with aspects of the curriculum they can become disengaged from them; in turn, low achievement can impact negatively on their self-esteem and motivation, thus hindering a positive relationship with self. Issues can be further complicated when a child has a combination of difficulties, for example a child with ADHD who also has dyslexia. Further, children who exhibit behavioural problems can find it challenging to form good relationships with others.

While this chapter has only scratched the surface of the range of difficulties many children face, you may be anxious about the challenges you may have in meeting the needs of those in your care. For children with SEN, there are strong guidelines in place which allow you to seek the specialist advice you, the children and their families need.

Every school and nursery is obliged to appoint one member of staff as a Special Educational Needs Co-ordinator (SENCO) who will work in line with the SEN Code of Practice (DfES, 2001). The Code of Practice aims to promote consistency of approach in meeting the special educational needs of children, allowing their voice to be heard in that process. A key focus is on prevention, so that those needs are identified as quickly as possible and action is taken. The roles and responsibilities for the local authorities (then local education authorities), governors, those in early education settings, maintained mainstream schools and special schools are laid out. There is also a strong emphasis on working in partnership with parents, the children themselves, and other agencies (DfES, 2001).

When practitioners have concerns, they should take either Early Years Action or School Action as appropriate. This move occurs when plans are needed that are in addition to those normally undertaken in the setting.

Individual education plans

Consultation with the SENCO is required, and an individual education plan (IEP) is written for the child. This includes:

information about the short term targets for the child, the teaching strategies and the provision to be put in place, when the plan is to be reviewed, and the outcome of the action taken. The IEP should only record that which is additional to or different from the differentiated curriculum plan that is in place as part of normal provision. The IEP should be crisply written and focus on three or four key targets.

(DfES, 2001, para 4:27)

It is essential that the construction of the IEP is done in discussion with both the parents/ carers and the child. IEPs are reviewed at least three times a year, where parents' views on the progress are actively sought. On many occasions, the child's progress against targets can be successful using only resources internal to the school.

However, it is sometimes necessary to bring in external agencies, which takes the procedure to the Early Years Action Plus or Schools Action Plus as appropriate. One such trigger (among others) for this next stage is if the child has emotional or behavioural difficulties which inhibit their own learning or that of others in the class (DfES, 2001, para 4:31). The school will approach the relevant agencies for consultation (for example, an educational psychologist or a social worker). These professionals may offer advice and/or undertake specialist assessment. The school continues to monitor progress on the IEP and if insufficient progress is made, the school may request a statutory assessment from the local authority if they have significant cause for concern about the child. The panel will examine the evidence provided by all parties. If they conclude that the child's needs cannot be *reasonably provided within the resources normally available to mainstream schools and early education settings in the area*, they may decide to grant the child a statement of special educational needs (DfES, 2001, para 8:2). Extra resources may be allocated to the school/ early years setting in order to provide additional assistance for the child.

Children with unidentified needs

As the Code of Practice (DfES, 2001) states, not all children with special educational needs will have had those needs identified in an Early Education setting or at a previous primary school. Teachers and Early Years practitioners may help to identify children who have special educational needs through a variety of means. These include measuring children's progress via assessments or being responsive to parents' anxieties.

CASE STUDY

An undetected special educational need

Sean was in Year 5 and was a highly motivated boy who worked conscientiously in most curriculum areas. His teacher noticed that his behaviour differed in many mathematics lessons, where he would be talkative, off-task and distracting others. She monitored his progress and realised that it was relatively low in comparison to his achievement in other subjects. When talking with his previous teachers, they simply commented that he didn't like mathematics and hadn't been motivated to work hard in it. Sean's teacher was not convinced and liaised with the SENCO and Sean's parents to explore the matter further. Eventually a specialist was called in, who identified that Sean had dyscalculia, which meant he had difficulties in working with numbers. The teacher adapted her teaching methods accordingly in mathematics and Sean's low-level disruptive behaviour ceased because the work was made more accessible.

Sean's case is typical of many children who have a learning difficulty which has not been identified and illustrates how easy it is to misunderstand a child's poor relationship with a curriculum area. Dyscalculia is one example of a learning difficulty which is not a behavioural difficulty *per se* but can lead to behavioural issues which are borne out of frustration.

REFLECTIVE TASK

Why did several teachers fail to suspect that Sean might have a learning difficulty in mathematics? How might some children actively hide their learning difficulties? How can the system improve the detection of special educational needs?

Inevitably, there are cases of children who do not receive the help they need. Some children are never identified as having a special educational need while in school, perhaps being simply considered as a late developer or a disaffected, unmotivated child. For some, this revelation has come later in life.

CASE STUDY
SEN in a young adult

Jenna is an undergraduate student taking a three-year QTS course. Although her performance in the classroom was rated very highly by her teachers and tutors, there was concern over the quality of her planning and her marks for written assignments which were low. A tutor referred her to the university's student support service who investigated her poor achievement in written work alongside external agencies. Jenna was identified as having dyslexia and was given appropriate learning support to enable her to manage the condition. Jenna said *It was tough but overall I am so relieved that someone had noticed my difficulties and taken action. I had always struggled with writing particularly at school and often copied my friends' work to avoid being noticed. I had been worrying that it would hold me back on my teacher training course but now I have coping strategies in place and my esteem has been raised. But it was tough – I struggled so much with my A levels that I never thought I would get on an ITT course and when I earned a place I was terrified that I wouldn't be able to cope. It has been a real journey.*

Jenna is not the only person who moved through the school system without having a special educational need identified. She was one of the fortunate ones who was able to maintain a positive relationship with the curriculum while she was in school, and was able to sustain a reasonably good relationship with self despite periods of self-doubt. Fortunately, the current generation of children is benefiting from a much greater awareness of frequently occurring needs, of sound guidelines for identifying and meeting those needs, and from more collaborative inter-agency working. While initial teacher training cannot fully prepare you for all the possible learning and behavioural difficulties you may encounter, it is important that you do your own research and attend continuing professional development courses. This action will help you in your important role of observing any potential signs of an undetected difficulty and being responsive to any concerns raised by children, families or colleagues.

> A SUMMARY OF **KEY POINTS**
>
> > The range of special educational needs is wide.
>
> > SEN can hinder the development of a child's relationship with self, others and/or curriculum.
>
> > You need to be aware of the current policies and procedures which support children with SEN or whom you suspect have SEN which have not previously been identified.

MOVING *ON* > > > > > > MOVING *ON* > > > > > > MOVING *ON*

This chapter has shown how you need to be aware of the range of special educational needs which some children have, and to be alert to those which have not yet been identified by others. The Core Standards develop this awareness further. During your NQT year, you will need to understand the roles of colleagues with specific responsibilities for children with SEN, disabilities and other learning needs (C20) and be able to judge when you need to draw on their expertise (C21, C25). This role will require a knowledge of the current legal requirements and national policies which are in force (C23). You also need to be able to identify potential child abuse or neglect and then follow the relevant procedures (C24).

With regard to your teaching, you will need to make effective personalised provision for all children, including those with SEN or disabilities to ensure inclusive teaching (C19). You may be working with teaching assistants who have specific responsibility for working with children with SEN. You are required to ensure that they fully understand their roles in supporting learning (C41).

The following chapter consolidates what you have read so far to bring you extra practical guidance on the key issues covered which are relevant to the classroom. Given that behaviour is so clearly a complex phenomenon, Chapter 7 aims to give you greater confidence in dealing with issues which might arise whilst on placement.

FURTHER READING FURTHER READING **FURTHER READING** FURTHER READING

Ayers, H (2006) *An A–Z practical guide to learning difficulties.* London: David Fulton. This book is a dictionary of commonly used terms related to the learning difficulties of children and adolescents. It is written for a wide audience and in addition to describing the features of learning difficulties, it highlights areas of controversy. It is to be used in conjunction with its earlier A–Z of emotional and behavioural difficulties: Ayers, H and Prytys, C (2002) *An A–Z practical guide to emotional and behavioural difficulties.* London: David Fulton

Child and Adolescent Mental Health Services (CAMHS). For more information, see: www.everychildmatters.gov.uk/health/camhs (accessed 12 December 2007). The site explains the structure of CAMHS in detail.

Clough, P, Garner, P, Pardeck, T and Yuen, F (eds) (2004) *The handbook of emotional and behavioural difficulties.* London: Sage. This is a detailed overview of themes which underpin the study of these types of difficulties. It explores, from an international perspective, the contexts and causes of EBD and strategies and interventions which are used. Areas of tension and development are highlighted.

DfEE (2001) *Promoting children's mental health within early years and school settings.* London: DfEE. This is a clear and systematic guide for a wide audience, including teachers, which offers descriptions of mental health disorders and case studies which will help you understand the disorders and help the children who have them.

REFERENCES REFERENCES **REFERENCES** REFERENCES **REFERENCES** REFERENCES

Ayers, H (2006) *An A–Z practical guide to learning difficulties.* London: David Fulton

Birkett, V (2007) *How to manage and teach children with challenging behaviour.* Wisbech: LDA

DfEE (2001) *Promoting children's mental health within early years and school settings.* London: DfEE

DfES (2001) *Special educational needs code of practice.* London: DfES

Jones, G (2002) *Educational provision for children with autism and Asperger syndrome: meeting their needs.* London: David Fulton

O'Flynn, S, Kennedy, H and MacGrath, M (2003) *Get their attention! How to gain the respect of students and thrive as a teacher.* Abingdon: David Fulton

Rooney, S (2002) Inclusive solutions for children with emotional and behavioural difficulties, in P Farrell and M Ainscow (eds) *Making special education inclusive,* pp 87–100. Abingdon: David Fulton

Westwood, P (2006) *Commonsense methods for children with special educational needs: strategies for the regular classroom.* Abingdon: RoutledgeFalmer

7
Ways forward

Chapter objectives

By the end of this chapter you should be able to:

- **implement some practical strategies to help children build a positive relationship with self;**
- **implement some practical strategies to help children build positive relationships with others;**
- **implement some practical strategies to help children build a positive relationship with curriculum.**

This chapter addresses the following Professional Standards for QTS:

Q1, Q2, Q3a, Q3b, Q4, Q5, Q6, Q7, Q10, Q14, Q15, Q18, Q19, Q20, Q22, Q25a, Q25b, Q25c, Q25d, Q30, Q31

Links to: mathematics; religious education (RE); spiritual, moral, social and cultural development (SMSC); personal, social and health and citizenship education (PSHCE); social and emotional aspects of learning (SEAL); Extended Schools initiative; Early Years Foundation Stage (EYFS).

Introduction

Sometimes it can be hard to see the links between theory and practice. It is not uncommon to hear trainees leaving their last university lecture prior to placement to say, *Thank goodness that's over, now I can get into school and really learn how to be a teacher!* This chapter helps you to further translate the theory of Behaviour4Learning into practical activities. It should be emphasised that there is no simple solution to some of the problems you will encounter. Teachers cannot be expected to solve all of the problems which children face in life – but there are practical steps which you can take to make a difference to their lives.

Hopefully you have seen that using behaviour management strategies alone is not sufficient to achieve high levels of good behaviour (Weare, 2004; Holmes, 2005). They are essential, but in this area of your job there are no 'quick fixes' because teaching and learning are complex affairs (Haydn, 2007). Behaviour4Learning is not simply another set of theories – it signposts those complexities of relationships and social knowledge and offers you strategies to understand behaviour in more depth.

Advice on developing children's positive relationships with self

In Chapter 3 you learnt that the main components involved in a child's sense of identity include self-efficacy, self-esteem, self-confidence and motivation. Enabling children to explore and develop their own sense of identity is a crucial part of SMSC and PSHCE, and a vast range of materials exists to support you in this task. The SEAL resources are invaluable to this end.

Frequently used activities relate to:

- asking children to explore their emotions;
- allowing children to identify what they are good at, and sharing that with others;
- giving children the opportunities to be involved in tasks which motivate them (perhaps through projects or non-fiction writing);
- assisting younger children in the school in various ways, for example through paired reading, which can raise older children's self-esteem;
- giving children positions of responsibility to increase self-confidence and self-esteem.

Advice on developing children's positive relationships with others

In order to develop the children's relationships with others, you will need to first focus on your relationship with them. This needs to start from the moment you first meet, often on a preliminary visit to the school. As you enter the school to meet your class, it can be overwhelming to stand in front a sea of faces. Getting to know the children by name should be one of your priorities as this will allow them to feel individually valued. It will also enable you to be more effective in your behaviour management – calling an off-task child by their name will have more impact than simply pointing at them or trying to attract their attention in other ways. Undertaking short games is a sound start to this end. Name activities include:

- playing games which are based around names (for example, use an adjective which describes your personality which begins with the initial of your first name such as Happy Harriet or Thoughtful Tom);
- children making name badges which include a drawing that depicts something they enjoy doing;
- making a class crossword with all of the children's names, and clues which describe their personalities.

If your remit allows, teaching children individually or in small groups in the first few days can be beneficial for getting to know several of the children personally before you work with them in the larger whole-class setting. For those of you undertaking a school-based training course such as the GTP, you will be in a stronger position to build longer-term relationships.

After the initial introductions, you will of course be building up relationships with the class. It is a good idea to do some activities in the very early stages of your placement which are focused on this aim. At the same time, some of these will enhance the children's relationships with each other. These tasks lend themselves to subjects such as literacy, RE, SEAL, PSHCE or SMSC (though not exclusively) and can be adapted to different ages. For example, you could ask children to:

- create a poem, booklet or poster about themselves;
- give a short presentation about a hobby;
- bring in items from home which are important to them;
- share their news after a weekend or a holiday.

You can also implement short, five- or ten-minute games which are designed to develop social and emotional skills and which can be done at any time of the day in between formal teaching. For example:

- children acting out emotions for others to guess;
- children co-operating in pairs, mirroring each other's actions;
- five-minute problem-solving activities done through group work.

Naturally, the children will also be eager to get to know you though you will have to ensure with upper Key Stage 2 children that their questions of you do not become too probing and personal. You need to always maintain a professional distance to avoid them treating you like an older brother/sister or an uncle/aunty. When you are teaching topics involving reflection, expression of feelings and sharing of opinions, consider:

- offering your view if appropriate, but ensure that you are not suggesting that your view is the right one (for example, if children ask you if you are religious);
- setting expectations that children will respect your views just as you will respect theirs;
- giving the children the right not to share if this is relevant to the task (for example, during circle time).

Children's collaborative skills

Children's social relationships will inevitably change over time. Some classes will appear to be more socially cohesive than others, often influenced by the personalities in the class. To nurture children's personal and social development and the ethos of the class, you can undertake different activities to build team work and collaborative skills. These can be done in all subjects and cross-curricular projects. For example, you can:

- give the children problem-based learning activities to solve as groups;
- ask the children to produce project-based booklets in groups;
- arrange team games in PE;
- play short games which involve co-operation, such as team quizzes.

Seating arrangements

The second report of the Practitioners on School Behaviour and Discipline, chaired by Alan Steer (2006), recommended that all schools should operate a seating plan. Seating arrangements can have a significant effect on children's relationships with their peers and also on behaviour. There are several factors to consider. Imagine, first of all, having to sit next to the person you most dislike each day, every day – how would that impact on your mood? Conversely, if you sat next to your best friends, would you be more likely to talk all day than concentrate on your work? The likelihood of the former is high – where children are allowed to choose who they sit next to, their social interactions can inhibit teaching and create misbehaviour (Steer, 2006). Children's personalities thus have a strong bearing on how seating arrangements impact on learning, but fortunately choice of seating is in the teacher's control.

As a trainee you are in a privileged position of being able to view the current seating plan objectively. You can often instantly see combinations of children which are not conducive to learning. When you are in charge of the class, you may be able to move children around – some children will be unsettled by a change to their routine but others will welcome it.

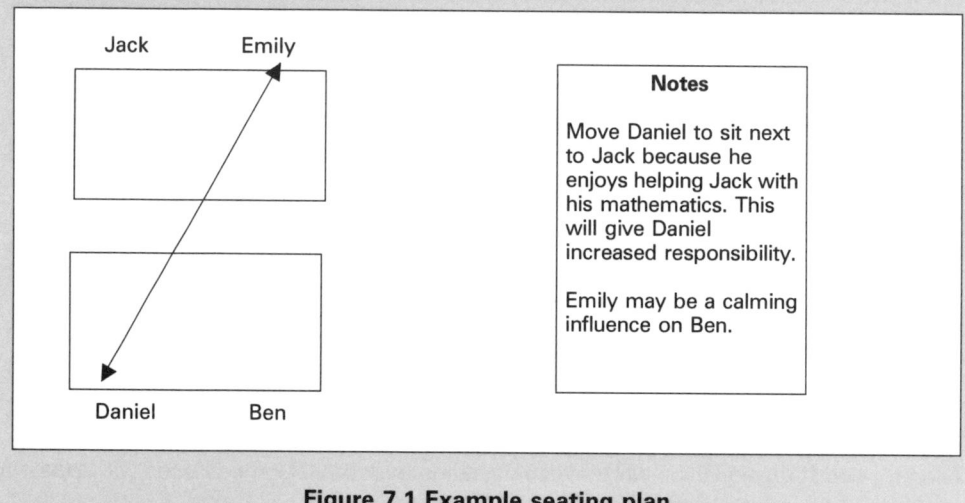

PRACTICAL TASK PRACTICAL TASK PRACTICAL TASK PRACTICAL TASK PRACTICAL TASK

Re-arranging the seating plan

Focus on the personalities of the children in your class. Can you see how different combinations of children might enhance behaviour for learning? Draft a plan and indicate who you would move and why. An example is given in Figure 7.1.

Jack   Emily

Notes

Move Daniel to sit next to Jack because he enjoys helping Jack with his mathematics. This will give Daniel increased responsibility.

Emily may be a calming influence on Ben.

Daniel   Ben

Figure 7.1 Example seating plan

Personality of the children is not, however, the only consideration. Wannarka and Ruhl (2008) reviewed the literature on seating arrangements and their effects on behaviour and academic attainment and found a lack of consensus as to the best formats. However, they concluded that the nature of the task and the type of behaviour sought should dictate the seating plan. For example, if you are asking the children to undertake independent work, you need to minimise their opportunities to talk to others and so seating in rows is ideal. If you are implementing an interactive task such as brainstorming, then clusters of tables appear to be more beneficial (Wannarka and Ruhl, 2008). Seating can thus have a significant impact on behaviour for learning and also has the potential to prevent some forms of disruptive behaviour. However, despite teachers' best attempts to improve social relations within a classroom, it is not possible to 'make' children like each other, so do not try to force this issue.

Relationships with children with emotional and behavioural difficulties

One of the most complex set of relationships you will encounter is that with children who have EBD. Visser (2002, page 68) describes a list of 'eternal verities' – core factors which underpin any intervention with these children; truths which arise from discussions, literature and research yet are not always made explicit. Visser (2002, page 75) offers a list of possible eternal verities. These are stated in Table 7.1 alongside a brief explanation where relevant, and an indication of your way forward.

Visser's (2002, page 75) eternal verities	Your way forward
Behaviour can change and emotional needs can be met	This belief drives professionals to help children with EBD. You need to maintain the belief that behaviour can change, and develop the emotional literacy of children in your class
Intervention is second to prevention	As you have seen, prevention needs to be the first priority. Ensure that you are as prepared as possible in all aspects of your teaching
Instructional reactions	Children with EBD are not always fully aware of the impact of their behaviour on others. This is potentially damaging for their relationships with others. You need to explain why the behaviour is inappropriate and offer the child alternative ways to react
Transparency in communications	Consistency in approach is paramount, as you have seen throughout this book. Play your part in maintaining this consistency and making it transparent
Empathy and equity	Empathy allows you to try to understand the behaviour of a child with EBD. If you can do this, you will strengthen your relationship with the child
Boundaries and challenge	All children need consistent boundaries but children with EBD need to have some flexibility, although the boundaries must not fail. Try to achieve this balance
Building positive relationships	Children with EBD can struggle at making and sustaining positive relationships because they regularly test boundaries. Ensure that you acknowledge this and provide a relationship for them characterised by emotional safety, personal involvement and trust
Humour	Having a sense of humour is essential

Table 7.1 Visser's eternal verities and their practical application

It is important to be aware of your responses to children with EBD in order to ensure that you adopt the most appropriate means of dealing with their behaviour.

REFLECTIVE TASK

When you have encountered a child with EBD who is disrupting learning, what has your response been? Were you angry? If so, why? Did you take time to explore the reasons for their behaviour? Did you consider how you could pre-empt such behaviour again?

Relationships beyond the school gates

As you have seen, the need to build relationships with parents/carers is fundamental for any school (Elton Report, 1989; Steer Report, 2005; Steer 2006, 2008). Schools need to reflect on their current policy and practice of liaison with parents, and identify ways of improving it. Seemingly small changes can be highly beneficial as they allow parents to feel increasingly involved, valued, and have their voice heard.

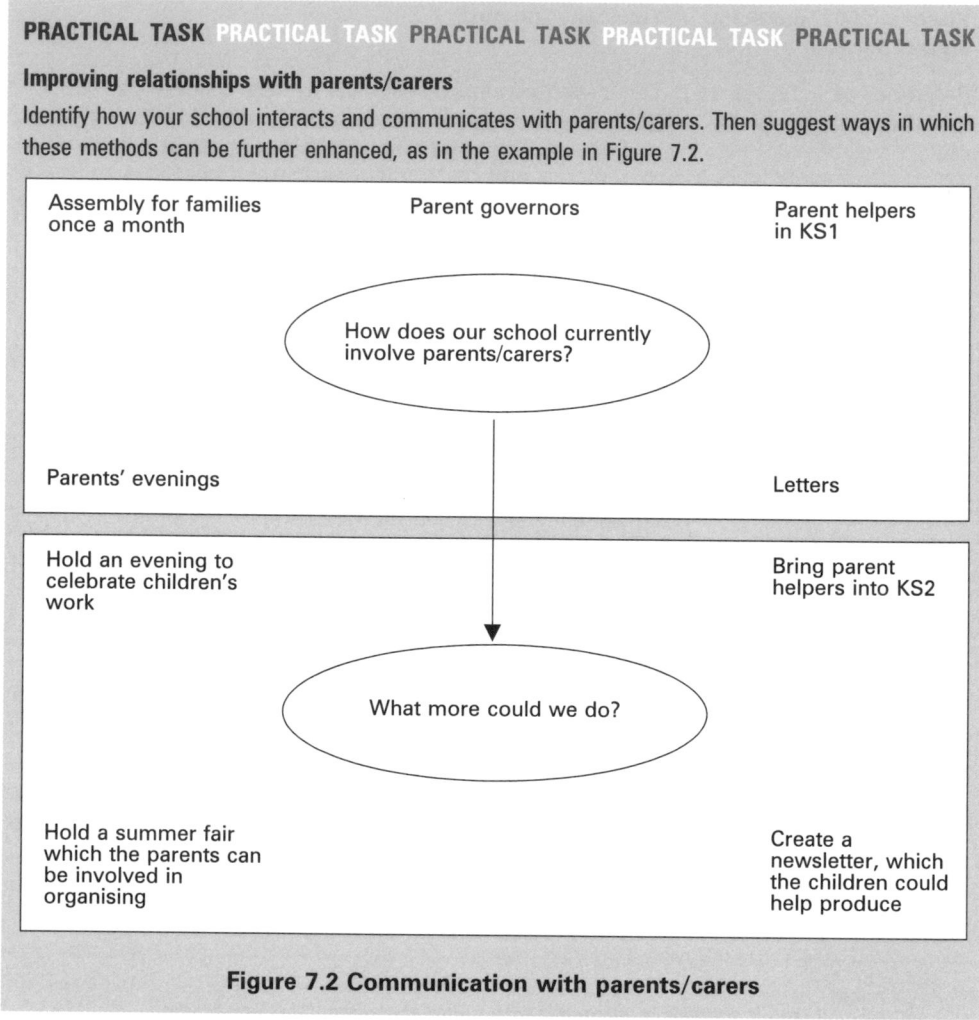

PRACTICAL TASK PRACTICAL TASK PRACTICAL TASK PRACTICAL TASK PRACTICAL TASK

Improving relationships with parents/carers

Identify how your school interacts and communicates with parents/carers. Then suggest ways in which these methods can be further enhanced, as in the example in Figure 7.2.

Assembly for families once a month

Parent governors

Parent helpers in KS1

How does our school currently involve parents/carers?

Parents' evenings

Letters

Hold an evening to celebrate children's work

Bring parent helpers into KS2

What more could we do?

Hold a summer fair which the parents can be involved in organising

Create a newsletter, which the children could help produce

Figure 7.2 Communication with parents/carers

The third paper in the review of behaviour led by Steer (Steer, 2008) addresses the importance of a school's relationships with parents. The report lists several initiatives or pilots which have been implemented in recent years to support parents in their parenting roles. These include: Family Intervention projects, New Parenting Experts, Parent Support Advisers, Sure Start Centres and Parenting Early Intervention Pathfinders. While initiatives need time to run before they can be adequately evaluated, it is good practice for you to investigate which projects are operating in your area. Steer (2008) makes recommendations for future practice which include the mapping of these initiatives. He also advocates the expansion of parent support advisers who work with the most disengaged or troubled pupils and parents in different ways, such as helping them access provision.

A key means of developing relationships with parents and other members of the community is through the 'extended school', as detailed in Chapter 4. Lewis (2006) suggests doing so in alignment with the sustainability agenda, which should also involve building sustainable communities. He cites examples of good practice, including schools that utilise their grounds by planting gardens in collaboration with other members of the local area, or who share in devising ways to reduce the school's carbon footprint.

In addition to designing projects, other ways in which to build community relationships include arranging visits out into the community, or inviting guests into school, as suggested in Chapter 4. Some further possibilities include:

- taking children to significant buildings in the locality for history/geography/RE;
- taking children to museums;
- taking children on a nature walk for geography/science, co-led by a local expert;
- taking children to the local fire station and/or inviting firefighters into school to demonstrate their role and the children's responsibility in keeping safe;
- inviting a local MP to talk to Key Stage 2 children for citizenship lessons;
- inviting local theatre companies to perform for children.

As a trainee you will not be required to take responsibility for such visits but you should take any opportunity available to learn about how visits are planned, and to accompany staff on any visits taking place.

Advice on developing children's positive relationships with the curriculum

As stated in Chapter 5, you can expect children to have preferences for different subjects. It is of course a challenge for you to engage children who dislike a subject. What practical advice can be offered? Firstly, there is generic advice. This relates to the point reiterated throughout this book, that teaching should be engaging. As you have seen, stimulating teaching involves a variety of components, including differentiation which is informed by assessment, a range of teaching strategies, appropriate pace of lessons and appealing resources. Teaching needs to be undertaken within an ethos of openness and respect.

Secondly, there is specific advice which is relevant to different subjects. Given that each of the curriculum areas has their particular difficulties and has so many topics, skills and concepts to cover, it is not possible to address them all. Instead, you will need to consult books, professional magazines and websites for rationales, advice and suggestions for stimulating activities in the areas you are finding challenging.

This section provides two in-depth case studies of trainees who encountered problems with children's behaviour when trying to teach specific areas of the curriculum. These particular examples have been chosen because they are challenging for many trainees and NQTs. Advice is given on how to improve the children's relationship with that particular programme of study but also raise points which are transferable to other curriculum areas.

CASE STUDY
No matter what I do, they can't tell the time!
Khalid was asked to spend four weeks in numeracy teaching a Year 2 class how to tell the time. He knew that the children had done some work on the topic before but a large number appeared to have forgotten what they had learnt previously. Khalid tried everything he could think of – numerous ways of explaining and utilising several types of resources – but he could not make progress with the majority. A small group, by contrast, were relatively advanced and could tell the time easily. By the second week, all of the children were restless and bored with the topic and were asking if they could do something else.

There is no point denying that this is a particularly difficult topic to teach even for the experienced professional. This is not surprising when you consider how many concepts are involved. Time is, of course, an abstract concept, and to understand a clock a child needs to have a good comprehension of multiplication, division and fractions. If they know that an hour consists of 60 minutes and are comfortable with the concept of division, they will be on their way to understanding that half an hour is 30 minutes and that a quarter is 15. But to calculate the latter requires the ability to either divide 60 by 4, or perhaps use an alternative method of calculation such as to halve 60 once then halve it again. It is common for many children in Key Stage 1 to grasp 'o'clock' and 'half past' but to remain at this stage for a considerable period.

Even before children embark on this challenging task of dealing with numbers, they need to have an understanding of the concept of time. Clemson and Clemson (1996) suggest practical work to convey the concepts of past, present, future and the passage of time – these are all necessary before a child can understand the concept of telling the time. The authors show examples of displays which children can make. These include the following.

- Drawings showing the sequence of the activities they undertake over the course of a day and a week.
- Making a calendar depicting the seasons.
- Marking the passage of time with chalk silhouettes drawn on the playground (Clemson and Clemson, 1996).

Khalid may have needed to 'go back' to these earlier stages before calculating how to tell the time on an analogue clock. It is tempting to assume that if children have been taught something before, they have retained and consolidated that learning. But particularly with topics that are not revisited regularly, it is natural for children to lose some of that information. Another complication for Khalid was that those who had mastered telling the time quickly took him by surprise. He had not anticipated having to move them on to digital time, and was thus initially unprepared for this level of differentiation. Always try to anticipate what the next stage of learning will be in your topic.

> ## CASE STUDY
> ### RE – what's the point?
> Lucy was finding it impossible to motivate the children in RE. She explained *The children just aren't interested in RE. I had to teach them about other world religions but it meant nothing to them because they don't live in a multicultural area and aren't from religious homes. They won't engage and they get bored and mess around.*

Lucy is not uncommon in facing difficulties in teaching RE and given that it is a statutory subject and has links with SMSC, it is worthy of attention. Lucy is aware that teaching needs to be relevant to children's lives but struggles to see how religion is relevant to those who are not religious and see little evidence of it in their neighbourhood. Lucy is not alone in this thinking and such an attitude will affect the quality of teaching, which is likely to be uninspiring and lacking in depth. In turn, children will not develop a constructive relationship with the curriculum area, as Copley and Walshe (2000, page 7) discovered when they asked 730 pupils aged 14–16 about their attitudes towards the Bible. Findings revealed that 30 per cent had had an initial negative reaction to it, with comments made such as it is 'boring', 'a waste of time', 'not true' and 'irrelevant'. Only 15 per cent reported a positive reaction and the remainder were either uncertain (27 per cent) or indifferent (26 per cent). These young people's views had developed from their years spent in RE lessons during primary and secondary education where, it would seem, they probably did not receive engaging and stimulating teaching. How did this happen?

A major difficultly in the teaching of RE by non-specialists is the misunderstanding of the aims and purposes of RE, particularly in schools which do not have a faith-based character.

PRACTICAL TASK PRACTICAL TASK PRACTICAL TASK PRACTICAL TASK PRACTICAL TASK

Can you state the purposes and aims of religious education?

This is a question which many trainees struggle to answer. You will need to consult your Local Agreed Syllabus to determine exactly what you need to teach, but most cover broadly the same ground. RE is generally split into two parts – 'learning about religion' and 'learning from religion'. QCA's publication *Religious education: non–statutory guidance on RE* (2003, page 8) outlines the main purposes of the subject and of these two components. 'Learning about religion' refers to:

- knowledge and understanding of religious beliefs and teachings;
- knowledge and understanding of religious practices and lifestyles;
- knowledge and understanding of ways of expressing meaning.

'Learning from religion' refers to:

- skill of asking and responding to questions of identity and experience;
- skill of asking and responding to questions of meaning and purpose;
- skill of asking and responding to questions of values and commitments.

QCA (2003) explains how these attainment targets aim to develop pupils' knowledge, understanding and ability to respond to the main principal religions present in Great Britain, so that they learn to understand and respect different beliefs, values and traditions (as well as ethical life stances) and their influence on societies. Further, children are encouraged to reflect on issues of meaning and purpose in life and on religious, moral and social issues. RE helps children to develop a sense of identity and belonging and thus has very strong links with Behaviour4Learning, SMSC and citizenship.

Lucy, like many trainees and qualified teachers, has struggled to understand the purposes of RE and this will affect any teaching she does in the subject, irrespective of the lesson's objectives. It is thus fundamental that all trainees are aware of their syllabus and of RE's aims. By the end of the Early Years Foundation Stage (EYFS), children *should have a developing respect for their own cultures and beliefs and those of other people* (DCSF, 2008, page 12), so work in this area begins with very young children. To have such a respect for other cultures and religions does not require an individual to be religious. To make aspects of RE relevant to non-religious children, you will need to find other points of relevance.

- When teaching about places of worship, begin by exploring the concept of places which are special to the children.
- When teaching about festivals, begin by exploring the celebrations which the children take part in.
- When teaching about religious founders, begin by exploring whom the children admire and why.
- Religions look at questions of meaning, purpose and value in life – questions which everyone asks, including children, irrespective of whether or not they are religious. For example: Why are we here? What

happens after we die? Why does suffering exist? Is there a God? You can also debate non-religious answers to these questions.

The inclusive school

This chapter closes with a return to the concept of the inclusive school because these offer many benefits in terms of children's relationships with self, others and curriculum. These schools offer a strong foundation in SMSC and PSHCE which nurture children's self-esteem and motivation through a strong community ethos and a stimulating and creative curriculum. Inclusion refers to all pupils, not just those with SEN, so you will need a good understanding of:

- all of the children's abilities;
- any special educational needs;
- the levels of children's social and emotional well-being;
- children's religious and cultural backgrounds.

The activities listed above which allow children to explore their own identity are useful ways of getting to know the children, as are whole-class projects which explore cultures and religions or issues affecting children. They also allow you to demonstrate the uniqueness of each child, and celebrate the diversity which exists.

A SUMMARY OF **KEY POINTS**

> **While there are no quick fixes to behavioural issues, there are practical steps that you can take to enhance relationships with self, others and curriculum.**

> **Short activities to develop social and emotional skills are a positive way to build relationships within the classroom.**

> **Understanding the underpinning philosophies of subjects, and of the concepts embedded in them, can help you to build relationships with curriculum more effectively.**

> **Developing relationships with others through increased communication and interaction will strengthen relationships with others.**

MOVING *ON* > > > > > > MOVING *ON* > > > > > > MOVING *ON*

As you move into your induction year, you will of course implement many practical strategies which will enable you to build strong relationships with the children and allow them to develop positive relationships with themselves, others and the curriculum. Many of the Core Standards relate to these areas. For example, you will need to establish fair, trusting, supportive and constructive relationships with the children (C1) and also collaborate with their parents, carers and your colleagues (C4a, C4b, C4c, C41). By promoting children's self-control, independence and co-operation via the development of their social, emotional and behavioural skills (C39), you will be empowering them to develop positive relationships with others.

To enable children to strengthen their relationship with curriculum, you will develop your professional knowledge of pedagogy by having an up-to-date knowledge of teaching and learning strategies (C10) and of curriculum areas and cross-curricular learning (C15). In order to offer personalised learning (C19) you will also need to know assessment requirements, approaches to assessment and to offer constructive feedback on children's learning so that they can develop further (C11, C12, C14, C32). Your careful planning, which takes account of assessment, can enable you to set appropriate learning objectives which allow children to consolidate and extend their learning (C26, C27, C28, C31). Through your encouraging children to reflect on their learning, they will be able to develop a sense of ownership (C33, C36).

In your role as trainee you should seek to identify as much good practice as you can with regard to building relationships. This will place you in a confident position for taking charge of your own class during your induction year. While the thought of that responsibility will excite you, it will probably also leave you feeling slightly anxious, but the following chapter reassures you that you have a wide range of support available to you during your training and induction.

FURTHER READING FURTHER READING **FURTHER READING** FURTHER READING

Briggs, S (2005) *Inclusion and how to do it: meeting SEN in primary classrooms.* London: David Fulton. This is a very practical guide to developing inclusive practice, giving advice on planning and teaching, working with families, social interaction and behaviour and working with children with learning difficulties.

Mosley, J, Sonnet, H and Cripps, M (2006) *101 games for better behaviour.* Wisbech: LDA. This book offers a range of short games and activities which help children to develop self-awareness, motivation, empathy, social skills and manage feelings.

Roffey, S (2006) *Circle time for emotional literacy.* London: Paul Chapman. This book explores the history of circle time and the concept of emotional literacy before detailing circle time activities. Foci of activities include personal communication, self-awareness, self-esteem, feelings, friendship as well as challenging issues such as loss, anger and bullying.

SEAL – Social and Emotional Aspects of Learning. Most schools will have the pack of materials which are designed to be used in schools. See the Social, Emotional and Behavioural Skills website for more information: www.teachernet.gov.uk/teachingandlearning/socialandpastoral/seal_learning accessed 20 October 2008.

REFERENCES REFERENCES **REFERENCES** REFERENCES **REFERENCES** REFERENCES

Clemson, W and Clemson D (1996) *Maths in colour.* Cheltenham: Stanley Thornes

Copley, T and Walshe, K (2000) The Bible in the upper secondary school: not always more boring than watching paint dry. *REsource*, 23(1): 6–8

DCSF (2008) *Early Years Foundation Stage.* Nottingham: HMSO

Elton Report (1989) *Discipline in schools. Report of the committee of inquiry.* London: HMSO

Haydn, T (2007) *Managing pupil behaviour. Key issues in teaching and learning.* Abingdon: Routledge

Holmes, E (2005) *Teacher well-being: looking after yourself and your career in the classroom* Abingdon: RoutledgeFalmer

Lewis, J (2006) The school's role in encouraging behaviour for learning outside the classroom that supports learning within. A response to the 'Every Child Matters' and Extended Schools initiatives. *Support for Learning*, 21(4): 175–81

QCA (Qualifications and Curriculum Authority) (2003) *Religious education: non–statutory guidance on RE.* London: QCA

Steer, A (chair) (2006) *Learning behaviour, principles and practice – what works in schools.* Nottingham: DfES. Available from www.teachernet.gov.uk/publications, accessed 7 July 2008

Steer, A (chair) (2008) *Behaviour review, paper 3.* Available from www.teachernet.gov.uk/docbank/index.cfm?id=12743, accessed 10 September 2008

Steer Report (2005) *Learning behaviour: the report of the practitioners' group on school behaviour and discipline.* London: DfES

Visser, J (2002) The David Wills Lecture 2001: Eternal verities – the strongest links. *Emotional and Behavioural Difficulties,* 7(2): 68–84

Wannarka, R and Ruhl, K (2008) Seating arrangements that promote positive academic and behavioural outcomes: a review of empirical research. *Support for Learning,* 23(2): 89–93

Weare, K (2004) *Developing the emotionally literate school.* London: Paul Chapman

8
You're not alone: your relationships with others

Chapter objectives

By the end of this chapter you should be able to:

- **understand the importance of a whole-school approach to behaviour;**
- **acknowledge the role of your relationships and their effect on your professional practice;**
- **understand the government's aim to ensure inter-agency working;**
- **know how to seek support from others.**

This chapter addresses the following Professional Standards for QTS:

Q3a, Q3b, Q4, Q5, Q6, Q20, Q21a, Q21b, Q32, Q33

Links to: Early Years Foundation Stage (EYFS); Every Child Matters (ECM); Code of Practice for Special Educational Needs; spiritual, moral, social and cultural development (SMSC); personal, social and health and citizenship education (PSHCE).

Introduction

You have already seen how important relationships are to children, and the impact they can make on behaviour for learning. For you, good relationships are also essential. This chapter looks at the professional relationships which you will develop that offer you support in your role as a teacher in general, and with children's behaviour in particular. It considers the practical and affective aspects of those relationships as you work as part of a team committed to delivering the Every Child Matters outcomes for children. Indeed, ECM's commitment to the five outcomes of staying safe, being healthy, enjoying and achieving, making a positive contribution and achieving economic well-being is attainable only through full co-operation between different agencies, parents, carers and families (DfES, 2004). For teachers, there is a wide support network in all areas of their role, including dealing with issues of behaviour.

As a trainee, you will always have colleagues around you ensuring that you are managing your commitments to the placement. The class teacher/mentor and other members of staff will be there to help and advise you on all aspects of your remit. With regard to behaviour management, they will explain individual children's needs to you and their most effective strategies for that class. Nevertheless, it can still be a daunting prospect, particularly in the early stages of your placements, when you are taking sole responsibility for the children's behaviour and learning in that lesson. Throughout this book, you have seen that learning and behaviour are inextricably linked, that careful planning will prevent many possible instances of misbehaviour, that strong identity, self-esteem, self-efficacy and motivation are fundamental to effective learning, that a child's strong relationship with self, others and curriculum are key components in determining appropriate behaviour for learning, and that inclusion of all children is essential. Throughout, and particularly in the previous chapter, you have been given practical advice on ways forward. Nevertheless, you can be forgiven for feeling overwhelmed with the task of empowering children to achieve positive behaviour for learning. This chapter reassures you that you are not alone when taking on this task and that, in addition to your colleagues within the school, there is also support from a wide range of other adults beyond the school gates.

A whole-school approach

As this book has demonstrated, a whole-school approach to behaviour is essential. If teachers operated their own independent systems in every class, there would be little consistency or continuity for the children. Children need routines, boundaries and clear expectations. If a school had a policy that children could not wear jewellery, but one teacher was more lenient and 'turned a blind eye' to those in her class who did, then children would rightly argue that that was unfair. Children have a strong sense of justice and are quick to complain if they perceive a situation to be unjust. Naturally, such circumstances can breed resentment and as a result, the other staff will have considerable difficulty in reinforcing the rule as they will constantly hear *but Miss Greene lets her class wear jewellery!*

Rogers (2005) states that if a whole-school approach is taken, behaviour can be significantly improved. A whole-school approach demands consistency (Ofsted, 2005; Steer Report, 2005), as you saw in Chapter 2. The key point for this chapter is that to achieve such consistency, every member of the school needs to play their part. This applies not only to teaching staff but also to any member of staff who comes into contact with children anywhere in the school, for example in reception, the dining hall or the playground. In your position as a trainee, you have a vital role to play in ensuring that the whole-school approach is maintained. Some children are likely to try to exploit your position and see how far they can 'push you', and you need to show them that you are a part of the school team. Further, if you implement the school policy, your supporting of the school will be reciprocated by your colleagues.

Support from colleagues in school

Trainees generally report excellent support from staff in school, although the amount and quality received can vary from placement to placement depending on its length, other staff commitments (such as an imminent Ofsted inspection) and the number of trainees in the school at that time. Naturally you will spend the largest amount of time with the class teacher. Even on placements which involve you taking most of the responsibility for the class, the teacher will be eager to ensure that you are fully prepared to teach the children to the best of your ability and provide continuity with the work and routines they have already set.

Hopefully you will have had placements in which you were fully integrated into the school, but sadly the degree of inclusion can vary. However, if you do find yourself in a similar situation to Joe, ensure that you remain professional, take the initiative at all times and focus on giving the children the best learning experiences that you can. Work together with other students in the school as much as possible, and with as many helpful staff who are willing to give their time.

The class teacher

> ### CASE STUDY
> **Too busy to have trainees**
> Amelia explained that her last placement had been incredibly supportive. Her mentor had given her time freely, the TA spent morning playtimes helping her with marking, the head teacher made time to informally review her progress and the secretary helped her to find policies. In contrast, Joe had not been so fortunate. His school had recently had a poor Ofsted inspection and morale was low. Joe felt that his teacher had not really wanted him there and his suspicions were confirmed when a member of staff said that the head had asked the university for students, despite staff saying that they didn't feel that it was a suitable time to have them.

For those placements where staff are able to give you the full support you need, you should still take a proactive role in seeking that support and also in responding to it; it is a two-way relationship. Teachers are very busy and while they will willingly sit and discuss your remit and progress through it, they also expect to see considerable initiative in you. A frequent reaction from many trainees is to be slightly reserved, which is often founded on a desire not to 'tread on the teacher's toes'. As a consequence they can sometimes hold back, not wanting to interrupt the teacher's busy schedule or distract them. While this attitude is borne out of the best of intentions, teachers often misinterpret it as a lack of initiative. To avoid this situation and to give your relationship with the teacher a stronger foundation, consider the following tips.

- Always remain professional – arrive early, don't leave when the bell rings, and be well prepared.
- Don't sit back and wait to be spoken to: offer your planning and seek feedback on it.
- Ask for informal feedback on your progress.
- Ask for access to relevant documents such as the behaviour policy.
- If you are struggling with behaviour management, do not try to hide it. Be honest and ask for advice.

Support from the SENCO

Within the primary school, the first point of contact for teachers who have concerns about a child is usually the Special Educational Needs Co-ordinator (SENCO). As detailed in Chapter 6, every school is obliged to appoint one member of staff in this role who will work in line with the SEN Code of Practice (DfES, 2001), as outlined earlier. The Early Years Foundation Stage (EYFS) states that each setting (excluding childminding settings) should have a named practitioner who is responsible for behaviour management issues. This person should be able to provide guidance to other staff and also access advice from experts if necessary (DCSF, 2008). If appropriate, it will be valuable to develop relationships with this named practitioner, so that you gain an insight into practice in the EYFS, even if you are working with older children. This will give you insight into the approaches to behaviour management at the beginning stages of a child's formal education.

PRACTICAL TASK PRACTICAL TASK PRACTICAL TASK PRACTICAL TASK PRACTICAL TASK

While on teaching practice, you should make contact with the SENCO and/or EYFS named practitioner and explore their role with them in depth. Focus on children's behaviour and ask them the following questions.

- What types of behaviour do they deal with?
- Which outside agencies do they collaborate with to address behaviour issues?

- What types of targets do they give children with behaviour difficulties?
- What are the practical problems they face in dealing with behavioural issues?
- How do they collaborate with parents?
- If relevant, what kinds of resources are provided for children with statements of special educational needs?

Support from your school-based mentor

Within the school you will be assigned a mentor, who is often in middle or senior management, and who will advise you on a range of developmental issues, including classroom management. They are there not only to advise, but to listen, motivate, empower, review, encourage reflection and act as a critical friend (Cohen et al., 2006). With your mentor you can discuss a variety of topics related to behaviour, including the school's approach to SMSC and PSHCE and how these impact on the children's behaviour for learning. You can also reflect on your contribution to children's self-esteem and motivation.

Support from your university-based tutor

Your university/institution-based tutor also has a significant role to play in your development in the classroom. This role manifests not only through preparation in seminars and tutorials, but also on their visits to school to observe you teach. Your institution will have a partnership agreement with the school which will make clear each partner's roles and responsibilities (Cohen et al., 2006).

Your tutor who visits you in school will, together with your class teacher and school-based mentor, encourage you to develop your skills as a reflective practitioner. As detailed in the following chapter, being a reflective professional demands that you are honest with yourself. You will need to enter into a genuinely open dialogue with your tutor on all aspects of your approach to behaviour. Your tutor will quickly be able to identify your style of classroom management but you may also need to be proactive in explaining the steps you have taken in your planning to prepare for positive behaviour. This is because it is not possible to detail all of your thought processes in your planning. These thought processes might include:

- justification of chosen teaching strategies which might have arisen due to the class's preferences;
- specific groupings which might separate children who do not work well together;
- activities designed to raise self-esteem;
- how you devised differentiated tasks at the right level to meet all the children's needs;
- how you ensured that children's comments and thoughts were valued;
- how your approach to the lesson complies with the school's relevant policies on SMSC or behaviour.

In addition to celebrating your thorough planning and your other successes on placement, it is essential that your dialogue with your teacher, mentor and tutor acknowledges your areas for development and your anxieties. Rogers (2005) argues that it is important to share experiences of 'failure' with other colleagues. In so doing, it highlights how all teachers have similar concerns, issues and problems. When colleagues are prepared to share such experiences it adds to a climate of openness in which problem-solving can take place. Support in social settings can help individuals cope with stress, and can take a variety of forms. Rogers specifies:

- *moral support – the demonstration of empathy and understanding;*
- *problem-solving support – which can help you find practical solutions to the difficulties;*
- *structural and instrumental support – whereby staff can identify areas for improvement such as poor playground management plans;*
- *collegial feedback and peer appraisal – good-quality feedback on your performance can help your self-esteem and professional development.*

(Rogers, 2005)

While it is tempting to try to hide weaknesses from a person who is assessing you, if you are struggling to engage a class in learning (for whatever reason), this cannot be hidden. There may well be a vast array of reasons why a particular group of children is disaffected, and some of these will not reflect badly upon you, provided that you are honest and can demonstrate what practical steps you are taking to try to engage them in learning.

REFLECTIVE TASK

Teachers, mentors and tutors are there to help you. How often do you actively ask for help? If you do this regularly, how does this make you feel? If you are reluctant to ask for help, why is this? How would your progress be different if you sought more support?

Support from parents, carers and families

As you have seen throughout this book, best practice includes regular collaboration and good communication with parents. ECM includes parents, carers and families in their plan to meet the five key outcomes, stating their expectation of them for each one. For example, in the outcome 'make a positive contribution', which includes children engaging in positive behaviour both in and out of school, the document expects that parents, carers and families will promote positive behaviour (DfES, 2004).

ECM's agenda is fully supported in new initiatives, including the Early Years Foundation Stage (EYFS) which creates a framework for partnership. A key focus is on positive relationships for children, which includes partnership with parents and carers. It recognises that Early Years practitioners need to work closely with parents in order to identify children's learning needs and to ensure a fast response to any areas of particular difficulty (DCSF, 2008).

The Steer Report (2005) states that parents and carers, pupils and teachers all need to operate in a climate of mutual respect – and that in order to maintain good behaviour, the support of parents is essential. Both parents and schools need to have a full understanding of their rights and responsibilities. For example, the Report recommends that schools should make clear to parents, pupils and staff that bullying is unacceptable and they should ensure that such behaviour is punished.

Primary schools have daily opportunities to make contact with many parents/carers at the school gate. These informal opportunities are invaluable. Most Key Stage 1 teachers walk the children to the school gate at the end of the day, which gives them the chance to develop relationships with their parents/carers. This relaxed setting is ideal for passing on positive comments about the children's achievements that day, and develops strong foundations for open dialogue which can be essential if problems later arise. While many Key Stage 2 teachers do not take their classes to the gate, often in order to encourage independence in the children, it is a good idea to follow the children to the gate, perhaps once a week, in order to build and maintain relations with the parents. As a trainee, try to accompany your teacher on this task. After all, the parents will be intrigued to meet you after hearing all about the 'new grown-up member' of the class from their child.

There are many other means of developing links with those involved in the children's home lives. Face-to-face meetings include sports days, school plays, leavers' ceremonies, trips, assemblies and of course parents' evenings. However, it is not only through face-to-face gatherings that liaison can be developed, and alternative means are essential given that some parents never attend school events. Additional means of communication include school newsletters, phone calls and letters about specific events or issues. Clear, regular and open communication can help to build respectful relations over time.

All teachers have to face difficult conversations with parents/carers at some time in their career and when the topic is a child's behaviour, the dialogue can be particularly sensitive.

CASE STUDY
A difficult conversation

Michael has taught for over 20 years. During that time he has had to talk to many parents about their children's unacceptable behaviour. *I am always anxious about such conversations*, he explained. *I often say to my friends that if I had a pound for every parent who said to me that they knew their child was no angel, but they would never hit another child unprovoked... well I could have retired a decade ago! Even if staff had witnessed the event, it is often impossible to convince the parent of their child's role in it. As cynical as this might sound, it seems to me that, according to parents, a bully always seems to belong to somebody else.*

Michael and his colleagues were committed to building relationships with parents and on the whole the school had achieved well, as noted in their Ofsted reports. His comments were borne out of frustration, and are indicators of how people can perceive a situation in different ways. The types of conversation he has had are inevitably sensitive because some parents/carers are upset at hearing what they perceive to be allegations against their children. While many will be co-operative, seeking to resolve the situation, others may not and the Steer Report (2005) advises that schools should ensure that all staff are trained in the skills required to deal with difficult parental conversations.

Support from other agencies

The government recognises that schools cannot solve all behavioural problems alone, and need specialist support from other agencies. Consequently, to ensure that the ECM agenda is met, there have been significant changes in the system of children's services. These include the integration of a wide range of services, so that professionals in different settings (for example, schools, social services, doctors) communicate with each other to ensure that a child's well-being is safeguarded. With strong leadership at all levels of the system, a shared responsibility across agencies should protect children from harm.

A Common Assessment Framework has been developed to provide a national process for early assessment to identify children's additional needs quickly and accurately. Such an integrated approach can offer effective support for children, as a case study published in ECM exemplifies. A mother had concerns that her young son's aggressive behaviour in nursery school would worsen over the summer holiday and she was worried that she would not receive the necessary level of support when he entered Reception class. The school undertook a Common Assessment with the mother and planned how a range of services could co-operate to support her son. These included an education welfare assistant, a health visitor and a teacher. The result was that the education welfare assistant worked with the child at home and at school, and the boy was also re-referred to a speech therapist. The health visitor offered behaviour support to his mother and the class teacher acted as the first point of contact for the family. This co-operation between different agencies resulted in the family feeling that they had support through a co-ordinated approach (DfES, 2004, page 19).

Like the boy in this ECM case study, many children will require more support for their behaviour than a school can offer alone. A wide range of professionals can be involved in managing children's behaviour. Mukherji (2001) outlines who they can consist of. As part of the primary health care team, who are based in local communities, general practitioners, health visitors, community midwives and community nurses are all key workers who are likely to be approached by parents who are anxious about an aspect of their child's behaviour. These approaches might be made when the child is young, possibly before they enter school. Other professionals who might be consulted depending on the type of concern raised include the school nurse, a pediatrician, psychiatrist, educational psychologist, clinical psychologist, speech and language therapist, occupational therapist, physiotherapist and social worker.

Support: feeling connected

PRACTICAL TASK PRACTICAL TASK PRACTICAL TASK PRACTICAL TASK **PRACTICAL TASK**

How do you feel when you are supported?

Think of a placement in which you have felt particularly well supported. How did this make you feel? See the example in Figure 8.1.

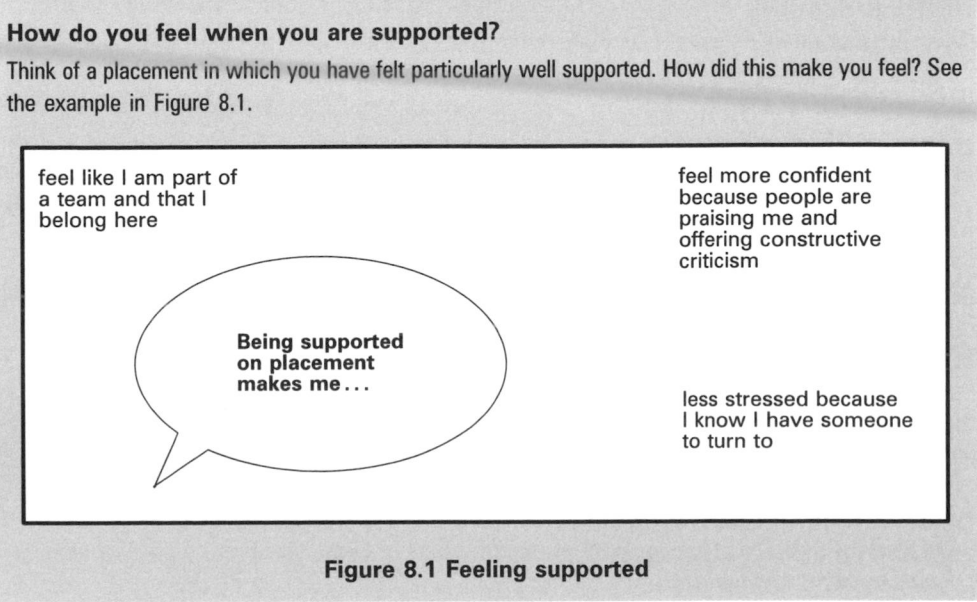

Figure 8.1 Feeling supported

When we feel unsupported, stress levels rise and panic is likely to set in – we can feel overwhelmed with the tasks facing us and at a loss at what to do when things appear to be going wrong. Conversely, when we feel supported, we have that sense of feeling connected to others, of being a part of a group, which is a key characteristic of spirituality. When belonging to a professional team, our motivation levels can increase. Fortunately, while your role on placement is a demanding one, you have these strong networks of support embedded, with those you work most closely with sharing your aim to gain your QTS award and develop into an effective teacher. Never be afraid to ask for help.

A SUMMARY OF **KEY POINTS**

> **As a trainee, your tasks may seem daunting but there is a wide network of support available to you.**

> **Trainees, NQTs and teachers alike are part of a team which extends beyond the school gate.**

> **Every Child Matters actively promotes inter-agency working to support children, and you are a part of that network.**

MOVING *ON* > > > > > > MOVING *ON* > > > > > > MOVING *ON*

Your ability to develop professional and core relationships is the first theme of the Core Standards. This includes relationships with the key people and agencies identified in this chapter (C4, C5) – as well as deepening your relationships with the children (C1). It will be essential that you are fully committed to working in a co-operative and collaborative style (C6) and recognise that you are a team member who should also share the development of effective practice with them (C40). Where children's behaviour is a concern and there is need for outside agencies, you should be able to determine when you need to draw on the expertise of colleagues (C21). To do so will require an understanding of the current legal requirements and national policies on the promotion of children's well-being (C22), as well as an understanding of the roles of colleagues such as the SENCO (C20).

The following chapter draws together many themes raised in this book in order to focus you on reflecting on and evaluating your own progress to date in the field of behaviour.

FURTHER READING FURTHER READING **FURTHER READING** FURTHER READING

Every Child Matters: change for children (2004) London: DfES. Read the ECM document to learn more about inter-agency collaboration. The document is available from: www.everychildmatters.gov.uk

Mukherji, P (2001) *Understanding children's challenging behaviour.* Cheltenham: Nelson Thornes. Mukherji details the roles of different external agencies who might be involved with children with behavioural difficulties. She also explores some of the therapies that are commonly used, including music, play, art and drama therapies.

REFERENCES REFERENCES **REFERENCES** REFERENCES **REFERENCES** REFERENCES

Cohen, L, Manion, L and Morrison, K (2006) *A guide to teaching practice.* Abingdon: Routledge.

DCSF (2008) *Early Years Foundation Stage.* Nottingham: HMSO

DfES (2001) *Special Educational Needs Code of Practice*. London: DfES

DfES (2004) *Every Child Matters: change for children*. London: DfES

Mukherji, P (2001) *Understanding children's challenging behaviour.* Cheltenham: Nelson Thornes

Ofsted (2005) *Managing challenging behaviour.* London: Ofsted

Rogers, B (2005) *A whole-school approach to behaviour management.* London: Paul Chapman

Steer Report (2005) *Learning behaviour: the report of the practitioners' group on school behaviour and discipline.* London: DfES

9
Self-reflection: how are you doing?

Chapter objectives

By the end of this chapter you should be able to:

- **describe the necessity of self-reflection in educators' professional development;**
- **develop your self-reflection skills with regard to your role in behaviour for learning;**
- **begin to systematically plan for your professional development in the area of behaviour for learning.**

This chapter addresses the following Professional Standards for QTS:

Q7a, Q7b, Q8, Q9, Q10

Links to: Career Entry and Development Profile (CEDP)

Introduction

Throughout this book reference has been made to your need to reflect upon your own practice and to develop it accordingly, and you have undertaken reflective tasks for that reason. This chapter takes an in-depth look at the concept of the reflective practitioner and how it affects your role, particularly in addressing behaviour for learning.

The reflective professional

Self-reflection is a key element of being an effective practitioner, and is a theme of the Standards for QTS and the standards beyond. To achieve QTS you will need to:

- reflect on and improve [your] practice, and take responsibility for identifying and meeting [your] developing professional needs (Q7a);
- identify priorities for [your] early professional development in the context of induction (Q7b);
- have a creative and constructively critical approach towards innovation, being prepared to adapt [your] practice where benefits and improvements are identified (Q8);
- act upon advice and feedback and be open to coaching and mentoring (Q9).

While these Standards apply to all aspects of your practice, they are highly relevant to your behaviour management. Reflective practice is a notion strongly influenced by the works of Dewey (1916, 1933) and Schön (1983). Dewey (1933) distinguished between routine action and reflective action. The former is guided by tradition, routine habit and institutional expectations. Practice in this instance is relatively static over periods of time, rarely changing. In contrast, reflective action demonstrates a willingness to engage in constant self-appraisal and development. In order to do this, an individual must be socially aware and flexible, and be prepared to undertake rigorous analysis of a situation.

Schön (1983) discussed the concepts of knowing-in-action and reflecting-in-action. Knowing-in-action refers to those actions we take and the judgements we make which we do spontaneously. Often we are unaware that we have learned these actions and simply 'do them'.

However, when reflecting–in-action, we consciously think about an activity while we are undertaking it.

In the classroom, there are many instances of practice relating to behaviour which we do out of habit. One example is the teacher who constantly shouts at a class to be quiet. This is a practice which can become habitual, yet has little effect. Apart from constituting bad practice – how do you feel if someone shouts at you? – if children become used to hearing shouting on a regular basis, it will not achieve the required effect. On the contrary, it usually serves to raise noise levels even further rather than reduce them.

Practitioners, including teachers, who encounter the same types of situations over and over again can develop a repertoire of expectations and techniques and the knowing-in-practice becomes increasingly automatic. It is thus important, as Loughran (2002) suggests, to question taken-for-granted assumptions. He emphasises that experience alone does not necessarily lead to learning, and that it is only by reflecting on experience that we can learn. As an example, we can explore the case of the teacher who shouts too much.

CASE STUDY
Bad habits
Jane, a teacher of ten years, constantly shouted at the children to behave. As a child, her parents had acted in the same way and she had unconsciously internalised their behaviour as being 'normal'. During an appraisal with the head teacher she was asked to reflect on her shouting and came to understand how she had developed this unproductive habit. To improve her behaviour management, she learnt more non-verbal management strategies. Over time, her practice changed with positive results for the classroom ethos and for the children's behaviour.

Identifying our routine action can be especially challenging because it is so ingrained. The language we use when we praise children is a simple way of exploring routine action as it is usually based on habit, and is influenced by our cultural practices. When I was working with trainees in Melbourne, Australia, I was immediately struck by their regular use of the word 'beautiful!' whenever a pupil had shown a piece of work, was sitting up straight, or had answered a question. This was a lovely word, delivered with a big smile and was quite uplifting. In the UK of course we are more likely to use 'well done' or 'good boy/good girl,' and these phrases are no more or less effective than the Australian 'beautiful'. However, if you used the word 'beautiful' in your classroom the children might respond with a few giggles. This example is used to show that the language we use is shaped by the society in which we live and hence we take it for granted. However, you need to be fully aware of the language you use because it is easy to inadvertently acquire unhelpful phrases which are exemplified in the commands you issue to children. As Chapter 2 showed, it is important to phrase requests positively rather than negatively, e.g. *please walk in the corridor* rather than *don't run*. If requests or commands are constantly framed negatively, this in turn will have an adverse impact on the atmosphere. You certainly don't want the children to perceive you as a 'moaning' teacher who is always complaining.

Ask a fellow student, TA or teacher to observe you at random times across a week and record the language you use when praising children and the language you use when giving them commands relating to their behaviour. A tally chart will give you an immediate overview of how positive or negative you appear in the classroom.

Reflection in collaboration

Bolton (2006) notes that reflection is often undertaken with another person, usually a tutor. While on teaching practice, you will be working with your class teacher, mentor and tutor on evaluating your progress. With them, you will have reflective discussions about your performance and will consider how best to move forward. Reflecting in collaboration is highly beneficial, as it allows you to gain from others' experience and advice, see yourself as others see you and view situations and ways forward that you might not have been able to do alone. There can, however, be difficulties in sharing reflections because people can have different perceptions of the same event. When someone else's assessment of a situation is different from our own, a degree of conflict can occur.

Perceptions

Chapter 1 highlighted the difficulties in classifying behaviour as low-level because individual teachers can have different reactions to children's behaviour from those of their colleagues. Further, the chapter also noted that teachers' definitions are not always fixed because other factors such as their mood can lead to different responses at different times.

Recognising your own perceptions of a situation is a key factor in ensuring that you develop as a reflective practitioner. It is potentially very easy for us all to continue working as we do if our practice seems effective. However, behaviour is a key area which highlights the need for reflexivity because, at the most basic level, the strategies which work effectively with one class are completely ineffective with another. Imagine you are faced with a class which has a higher level of disruptive behaviour than that of your previous one. You may feel helpless and desperately search for alternative strategies, doubting your ability to maintain control. It is essential that you explore your own views as to why this is the case, but it is equally important to seek the opinions of others too.

REFLECTIVE TASK

What explanations have you heard in schools for disruptive behaviour? Did you agree with the teachers' reasons? Were there alternative ways of accounting for the children's misbehaviour?

Teachers' views

Watkins and Wagner (1988) argue that teachers' explanations reflect a variety of influences. For example, they might reflect the teacher's personality. But they are also, to some extent, shaped by the context in which they are stated. Comments you have heard in the staffroom might largely be a release of stress from the previous lesson, and are unlikely to be repeated in other situations. Explanations given to an Ofsted inspector might be quite different.

Watkins and Wagner (1988, page 12) cite explanations for children's misbehaviour which are often used by teachers. They include the following.

- *They're that sort of person.*
- *They're not very bright, can't cope with the work.*
- *It's their age.*
- *This is a difficult neighbourhood.*

It is possible that the comments you have heard in school fit into these categories.

Children's views

Discussing teachers' perceptions gives us only one part of the story. Consequently, it is also important to explore children's views. Tattum (1982, cited in Watkins and Wagner, 1988, page 30) discussed pupils' reasons for their own misbehaviour in a special unit. Pupils said that: instances had been the fault of the teacher, the teacher had treated them disrespectfully, rules had been applied inconsistently, it was the fault of the school system and that they were only messing around. The findings which relate to placing the teacher at fault bear an interesting relationship to more contemporary research on children's perceptions of the characteristics of an effective teacher.

The Hay McBer report for the DfEE gathered the views of eight-year-olds who valued teachers who listen, encourage, believe in individuals, help them and make them feel clever (Hay McBer, 2000). Similarly, Haydn (2007), as described in Chapter 4, found that children rate teachers who are 'friendly' and 'talk to you normally' and offer praise as those most likely to inspire learning. For the children in these studies, it is clear that personal qualities in a teacher and their relationship with that teacher are of fundamental importance.

A child's perception of why they misbehave might thus be quite different from that of a teacher: a child might feel that the teacher does not listen to them, while the teacher might say that the child is from a difficult background. It is not simply a case of either the teacher or the child being right or wrong. A child might be using a teacher as a scapegoat to 'justify' their bad behaviour; a teacher might be blaming a child's home life when in fact they are largely at fault for not having developed an affirming relationship with the child or perhaps setting work that was not matched to their ability. There may be a complex set of reasons for why a child misbehaves – but you should always acknowledge that different people involved in the same situation can have quite diverse perceptions of it. These differing interpretations might mean that while you sincerely believe that your behaviour management is excellent, others might not. Sometimes the others might be correct. Sometimes there needs to be a compromise to meet on middle ground.

Increased self-awareness: a health warning

Becoming increasingly self-aware can bring about significant changes, both internal and external. It can give us insights into ourselves, into our motivations and behaviour and our subconscious thought processes. However, Rogers (1980) warns that it can be a potentially threatening and painful process.

CASE STUDY
Taking criticism

Lana had a difficult first placement in a Year 5 class, which had impacted negatively on her self-confidence. Her university tutor had failed her lesson observation, and the class teacher had been in agreement that Lana was seriously struggling. Both felt that Lana had not recognised the importance of planning and its links with behaviour. Further, her repertoire of behaviour management strategies was very weak and the children were constantly off-task, answering back, and little learning was taking place. Lana's initial response to failing the placement was to blame the children and the teacher. She maintained that the children were used to indiscipline and hence she could not impose discipline upon them. Lana was adamant that she was not at fault and felt angry that she was being accused of incompetence by a teacher who she believed had many failings. However, when a similar situation arose in a different school she was forced to take a closer look at her practice and gradually became more willing to see herself through others' eyes.

The path of becoming more reflective is never smooth, though it is less bumpy when you receive considerable praise combined with constructive criticism. It is also less bumpy when your self-evaluations concur with those of your mentors. However, when there is significant discrepancy between your views and those of others, there can be many psychological obstacles to overcome. Naturally there may be times when an observer's view is not necessarily right, and may be tainted by a hidden agenda, or contain a degree of projection by which they subconsciously 'project' their own faults onto you. Equally, your positive self-evaluation may not be entirely realistic . . . the complexity of people's construction of reality can often cloud the issue.

PRACTICAL TASK PRACTICAL TASK **PRACTICAL TASK** PRACTICAL TASK **PRACTICAL TASK**

Reflecting on a situation

The next time you encounter a behavioural issue, seek the views of an adult who was present and, when the situation is resolved, the explanation of the child. List the observations on a grid similar to the one in Figure 9.1. If the views differ, consider the possible reasons for each person's views. For example, if you think that a class behaved very badly but the teacher reassures you that it was not as disastrous as you thought, what can account for this discrepancy? Could it be because you are a perfectionist and expected the children to demonstrate faultless behaviour? Or is the teacher being overly generous because he doesn't want to dent your confidence?

Your development as a reflective practitioner

As you progress through your teaching practices towards QTS, you will become increasingly familiar with the processes of self-reflection. In time, as you look back at your performance on your first teaching practice, you should see be able to see how much you have developed. This is similar to re-reading an essay you wrote in your first year of your degree, and comparing it with a final-year essay – during your first year you may have been convinced that your work was worthy of a higher mark. By reading it again with the benefit of two further years' essay-writing experience, you should now see why it had not warranted a higher grade. Of course, your academic writing skills would have progressed

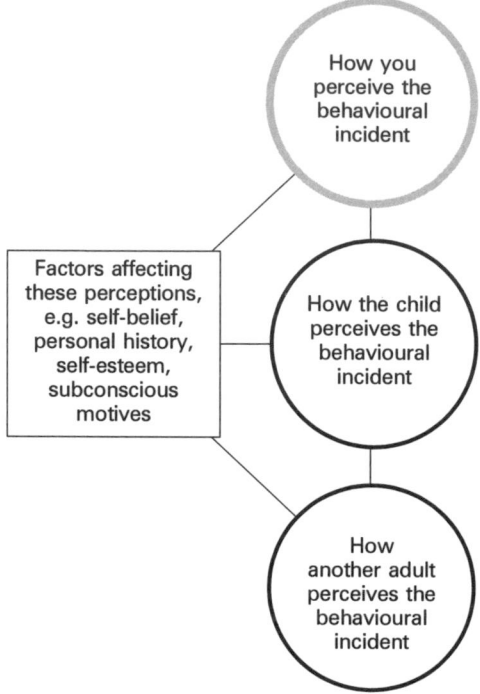

Figure 9.1 Perceptions of a situation

significantly only if you had responded to your tutors' constructive criticism and reflected on your own practice.

To aid you in your development as a reflective practitioner, you will be required to complete a Career Entry and Development Profile (CEDP). This is primarily an online resource aimed at trainees and NQTs which encourages you to identify your achievements and goals and discuss your professional development needs. It is structured around three transition points, with the first one being towards the end of initial teacher training, the second at the beginning of induction, and the third towards the end of induction. The TDA provides more information, including guidance notes, questions and sample formats on their website (at www.tda.gov.uk). As noted above, this reflection is done in collaboration with others, and the requirements for initial teacher training state that ITT providers must ensure that you are supported in completing your CEDP.

Writing plans is part of the reflective practice, which is cyclical in nature (Frecknall *et al.*, 2007; Pollard *et al.*, 2008). As Frecknall *et al.* (2007) observe, during your school practice, you will need to:

- identify and prioritise your areas of strength and weakness;
- create a personal action plan which addresses those identified areas and includes measurable targets;
- implement those plans while in school;
- record your actions and your evaluations of how well you have met your targets;
- review your progress with a mentor;
- set future targets.

The cyclical form of this process is clarified in Figure 9.2.

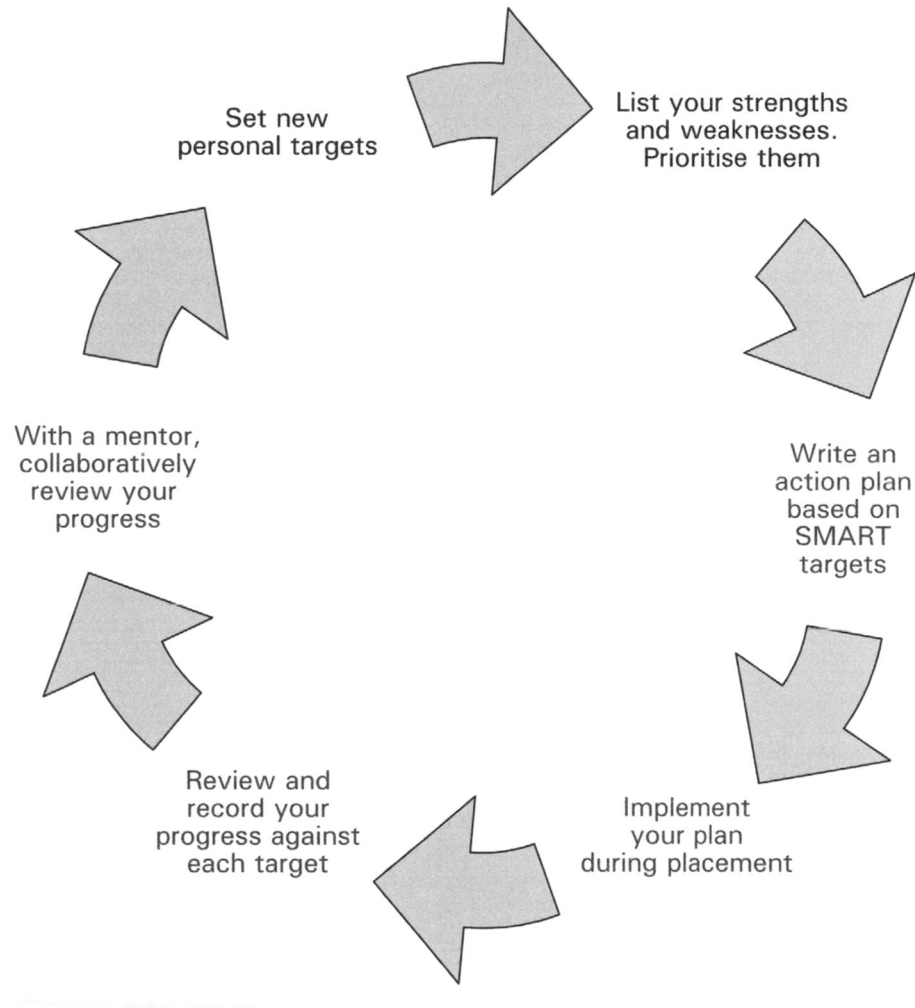

Figure 9.2 The cyclical nature of reflective process (adapted from Frecknall *et al.*, 2007)

Pollard *et al.* (2008) note that it would be impossible to reflect upon all of your activities in such depth all of the time, and emphasise that you should use them as learning experiences and apply what you have learnt in new and routine situations in the future.

The close links between behaviour and learning mean that you will need to constantly evaluate the two in conjunction with each other. A good starting point is when, at the end of each lesson, you evaluate its strengths and weaknesses in order to influence your future planning. When doing so it is essential that you explore your good practice with regard to behaviour as well as the times when it feels like a disaster. Take care not to simply describe what happened, but also to analyse *why* the components of the lesson were effective or less effective.

PRACTICAL TASK PRACTICAL TASK PRACTICAL TASK PRACTICAL TASK PRACTICAL TASK

When behaviour was good

Complete the grid below, to help you analyse how your teaching and behaviour management are combined. An example is offered for you.

Subject, theme of lesson and L.O.	Why behaviour was good and learning was effective	What could I do to be more effective next time?
Literacy/history – the Ancient Greek myths L.O: to produce an alternative ending to a Greek myth	The children were attracted by the Minotaur and the illustrations in the book were appealing. Children had the opportunity to be creative by writing their own ending to the myth – this gave them ownership of their work. The lower-ability group were supported with a writing frame which avoided them feeling pressured to write large amounts. Several 'new endings' were read at the end, offering a variety of tasks in the course of the lesson, and also allowed for positive feedback.	I would employ more creativity at the beginning. Rather than simply reading the story, I would ask children to read parts aloud together. This would engage more interest from those who lack concentration in listening. I would experiment with collaborative endings – children could act out their endings and a scribe in each group could write them down. This would enable lower ability children to contribute ideas without the pressure to write themselves.

When behaviour was bad

Now complete the following table, detailing a lesson in which the children's behaviour was less desirable. As before, an example is offered for you. Even though you are focusing on a weaker lesson, still include its positive aspects.

Subject, theme of lesson and L.O.	Why behaviour was poor and learning was not effective	What could I do to be more effective next time?
Maths. Fractions. L.O: understand that four quarters make a whole	My introduction was clear, and I used large pictures of shapes divided into quarters so that all children could see. Children were attentive. However, several messed around when collecting the plastic resources, treating them as if they were toys. One group finished the task in their workbooks very quickly and were bored, and started to distract others. Most of the class were talking in the plenary even though I was praising the work of the red group.	I had used an exercise in the children's textbooks as I thought that familiarity with resources would aid them. However, on reflection, this exercise was very short and not inspiring. The children could not see the relevance of knowing quarters and next time I would use a different teaching method for the main task – while the plastic shapes were good for making the task concrete, it lacked relevance. I might use biscuits or cakes next time to demonstrate that fractions are relevant for sharing in daily life.

Writing targets

Your lesson evaluations are one valuable means of identifying your own strengths and areas for development. You will also need to examine your practice outside of your teaching. You might, for example, recognise a weakness in developing relationships with parents or building a strong class ethos. Your evaluations can feed into your personal target setting, and some of these will inevitably relate to children's behaviour. All targets, irrespective of their focus, need to be SMART:

- Specific;
- Measurable;
- Achievable;
- Realistic;
- Time bound.

PRACTICAL TASK PRACTICAL TASK PRACTICAL TASK PRACTICAL TASK PRACTICAL TASK

Discuss the targets below with a friend. Are they specific, measurable, achievable and realistic? If not, why not?

1. To improve my behaviour management.

2. To increase my repertoire of non-verbal behaviour management strategies.

3. To give children more self-esteem.

4. To have better relationships with the children.

5. To create a more respectful ethos in the classroom.

Target-setting – be honest

CASE STUDY
The class behaved perfectly for me!
Margaret had been a teacher for over 30 years and primarily worked with children with social and emotional difficulties. She was skilled at developing a strong ethos based on mutual respect, and nurturing children's self-esteem. Building routine into the children's lives contributed to helping the children feel safe and demonstrate positive behaviour for learning. She explained, *the environment was rather fragile though, and was easily disturbed by even a minor change in routine. The appearance of a supply teacher was a significant trigger for poor behaviour because the children were unsettled. It did not make much difference how competent the supply teacher was. But I was always bemused when the supply teacher would report to my colleagues that the children had behaved wonderfully for them. My TA would confirm that the children most certainly had **not** been on their best behaviour! It is as if these experienced teachers felt that they could not admit that they had been unable to manage the children's behaviour for one day . . . the truth is, no one in the school would have judged them badly and would rather they had been honest and sought help.*

The setting of targets demands honesty with both yourself and your mentors. This can be a difficult task. Often the most uncomfortable question in a job interview is *What are your weaknesses?* – sometimes phrased as the less confrontational *What are your key areas for development?* A sense of panic can descend over the candidate. After all, if you regularly struggle to achieve positive behaviour in children, you won't want to admit to it because while it demonstrates honesty, you won't get the job. At the same time, you need to provide a constructive answer to show that you are a reflective practitioner and also to acknowledge that you are human – we all have areas in our professional performance which are in need of development. Children's behaviour is a particularly sensitive issue when it comes to reflective practice.

PRACTICAL TASK PRACTICAL TASK PRACTICAL TASK PRACTICAL TASK PRACTICAL TASK

Behaviour: How are you doing?

Finally, set yourself personal targets in relation to children's behaviour. You may wish to consult the TDA's guidelines for completing your CEDP to give additional support. Some questions you may wish to ask yourself include the following.

- Are you relying on the same set of behaviour management strategies and need to gain additional ones?

- Do you rely on your voice for managing behaviour – are there more effective ways to achieve the same goal?

- Is your differentiation sufficient so that all children are working at their own level and remain purposefully on task?

- Do some children misbehave because they have low self-esteem – what can you do to help increase it?

- Are you providing tasks which are suitably motivating?

- Do children feel as if they are part of a community, both in school and outside – if not, how can you increase that sense of belonging?

By focusing on your strengths and areas for development, and reflecting on your own performance and on how others perceive it, you can begin to formulate your own path for professional development. This can include observation of peers, being observed, attendance at continuing professional development courses and further reading. Taking responsibility for your own professional development will ultimately result in personal growth and increased self-efficacy, self-esteem, self-confidence and motivation, thereby strengthening your relationship with self.

A SUMMARY OF **KEY POINTS**

> **Reflective practice is an essential part of your professional development in training and beyond.**

> **You will be supported by mentors in your development as a reflective practitioner.**

> **When reflecting upon children's behaviour, remember that behaviour and learning are closely linked.**

> **Set targets for yourself which are SMART.**

MOVING *ON* > > > > > > MOVING *ON* > > > > > > MOVING *ON*

Throughout your professional life as a teacher, you will be required to constantly review your practice and identify and implement ways in which it can become increasingly effective. In so doing, you will be able to impact more fully on children's learning, attainment and well-being (C35). This review cycle will involve you evaluating your performance and improving your practice through professional development (C7); by acknowledging your areas for development and your strengths, you will be able to seek appropriate training courses to attend. Adapting your practice and approaches is also necessary in order to increase your constructively critical approach towards innovation (C8). You will need to maintain an open-minded approach to coaching and mentoring, and to act upon advice and feedback (C9).

The final chapter helps you to reflect on the contents of this book, summarising key points, and helping you to enter the classroom with confidence in relation to behaviour for learning.

FURTHER READING FURTHER READING **FURTHER READING** FURTHER READING

Pollard, A (2000) *Readings for reflective teaching.* London: Continuum. This book provides valuable readings from key texts on reflective practice.

Pollard, A, Collins, J, Simco, N, Swaffield, S, Warin, J, Warwick, P and Maddock, M (2008) *Reflective teaching: evidence-informed professional practice.* London: Continuum. You can gain free access to key extracts and diagrams from Pollard et al.'s work from www.rtweb.info/

TDA's website offers practical advice for the completion of your Career Entry and Development Profile. See: www.tda.gov.uk and enter 'CEDP' into their search engine to link to the various supporting pages.

REFERENCES REFERENCES **REFERENCES** REFERENCES **REFERENCES** REFERENCES

Bolton, G (2006) *Reflective practice: writing and professional development.* London: Sage Publications

Dewey, J (1916) *Democracy and education.* New York: Free Press

Dewey, J (1933) *How we think: a restatement of the relation of reflective thinking to the educative process.* Chicago: Henry Regnery

Frecknall, P, Dunne, U and Leedham, B (2007) Managing the learning environment, in K Jacques and R Hyland (eds) *Professional studies: primary and early years.* Exeter: Learning Matters

Hay McBer Report (2000) *Research into teacher effectiveness: a model of teacher effectiveness.* London: DfEE.

Haydn, T (2007) *Managing pupil behaviour: key issues in teaching and learning.* Abingdon: Routledge

Loughran, J (2002) Effective reflective practice: in search of meaning in learning about teaching. *Journal of Teacher Education,* 53(1): 33–43

Pollard, A, Collins, J, Simco, N, Swaffield, S, Warin, J, Warwick, P and Maddock, M (2008) *Reflective teaching: evidence-informed professional practice.* London: Continuum

Rogers, C (1980) *A way of being.* London: Continuum

Schön, D (1983) *Educating the reflective practitioner.* San Francisco: Jossey Bass

Tattum, D (1982) *Disruptive pupils in schools and units.* London: John Wiley. Cited in C Watkins and P Wagner (1988) *School discipline: a whole school approach.* Oxford: Basil Blackwell, p30

Watkins, C and Wagner, P (1988) *School discipline: a whole school approach.* Oxford: Basil Blackwell

10
Conclusion

Chapter objectives

By the end of this chapter you should be able to:

- **recognise the complexities of the three key components of the Behaviour4Learning approach;**
- **understand the need for behaviour management strategies combined with the Behaviour4Learning approach;**
- **suggest ways forward for dealing with behavioural issues;**
- **consider the implications for future research, policy and initial teacher training.**

This chapter addresses the following Professional Standards for QTS:

Q1, Q4, Q5, Q6, Q7, Q8, Q9, Q10, Q15, Q31, Q32

Links to: Spiritual, moral, social and cultural development (SMSC); personal, social and health and citizenship education (PSHCE); Every Child Matters (ECM).

Introduction

This book has demonstrated how complex children's behaviour is. Nevertheless, if you consistently expect children to always be quiet outside of discussion-based tasks, be polite, put their hand up and to remain on task, then you are taking the right approach by setting high expectations. Low-level disruptive behaviour will always occur, especially on a wet Friday afternoon when concentration is low and energy has not been expended, but you can minimise poor behaviour and develop nurturing relationships which will maximise children's positive attitudes towards learning. This chapter emphasises the salient points made throughout the book and poses new questions for you to reflect on as you move on through your training.

Behaviour management strategies

In line with the Standards for achieving QTS, you need to develop a repertoire of behaviour management strategies which will maximise good behaviour. As detailed in Chapter 2, some of these strategies are almost invisible to the untrained eye – sound preparation and planning, a brisk pace of lessons, appropriately differentiated and stimulating activities implemented through a variety of teaching methods.

You will have consciously thought about how you present yourself to the class, conveying a sense of authority which is not dictatorial. You will contribute to the development of the class ethos which will engender respect, tolerance and an openness in which children feel safe to share their views. In line with the school's behaviour policy you will also use a range of strategies to manage behaviour – including rewards and sanctions, games and signals to encourage quietness and tidiness and to attract attention.

You will have done all of these things, and still some children will engage in disruptive behaviour, albeit mostly of a low-level nature. This is why the Behaviour4Learning approach is fundamental as it enables you to explore the interacting cognitive, social and affective variables which influence a child's behaviour for learning.

Behaviour4Learning

In Chapters 3 to 5 you have explored the three key components of the Behaviour4Learning approach, which are:

- relationship with self (engagement);
- relationship with others (participation);
- relationship with curriculum (access).

It is worth repeating the illustration (Figure 1.1) which depicts the conceptual framework so that you can reconsider it in light of your reading of this book. It is repeated here as Figure 10.1.

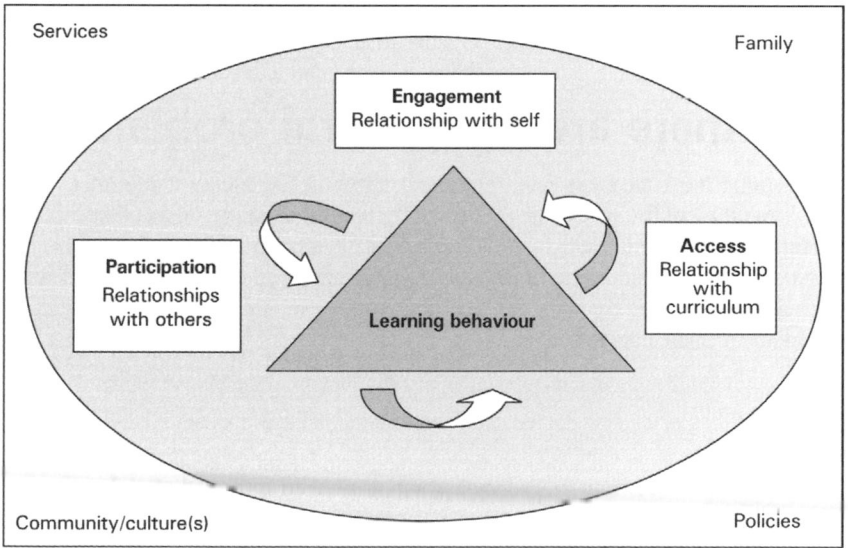

Figure 10.1 The Behaviour for Learning conceptual framework
Diagram taken from the EPPI-Centre Report (2004)

As the figure shows, relationships with self, others and curriculum do not develop in isolation and there is a considerable degree of overlap and complexity. Further influences include relationships with family and the wider community and culture(s), services and policy. As this book has detailed, many factors can influence a person's behaviour for learning, which means that there are no simple solutions to behavioural issues. For example, it is not easy to succinctly describe our identity as it is shaped over many years, comprises different components such as self-esteem and self-confidence, and has many influences both internal and external. However, by understanding the components and their complexity, and by exploring those in yourself, you can gain insight into how they work in children and how they affect their behaviour for learning.

To maximise your effectiveness you will need to implement behaviour management strategies alongside the Behaviour4Learning approach. B4L is not simply theory: it relates social, cognitive and affective theories to how children's attitudes towards learning are shaped and how these affect their behaviour for learning. If you understand how these influences arise, interact and work, you will gain valuable insights into why some children display negative attitudes towards learning which are evident in their behaviour.

Emphasising the person

There has been regular reference to SMSC and PSHCE in several chapters of this book. Although PSHCE is non-statutory, both areas are absolutely fundamental to understanding relationships. You are educating the 'whole child' – you are working with young people. Concerns about teacher retention rates and stress in both teachers and children to produce ever-higher academic results have highlighted the importance of the person in the teaching and learning process. All involved – staff and children alike – need to feel that they belong; that they are connected to others, to self and can fully relate to the curriculum that they engage with. Your work with SMSC and PSHCE will nurture those relationships and impact on behaviours for learning.

But still there are behavioural problems...

Behaviour management can be one of the most frustrating aspects of teaching, particularly if you have followed all of the advice given to you by teachers, tutors and authors. It is easy to be disheartened if you continually face disruptive behaviour in children. However, now you have gained a fuller understanding of Behaviour4Learning, you should be able to offer ways forward for a situation that trainees can find themselves in. Read the following case study and undertake the tasks that follow it.

> ## CASE STUDY
> **Why do I bother?**
> Ed was on his final placement in a school which appeared to have little social cohesion. The children in his Year 6 class were low in motivation. *I can't see why. My planning is clear, I've incorporated differentiation and used many different teaching strategies but a large number won't engage with learning. They won't even sit quietly while I try to introduce lessons. It's wearing me down because I am working every evening on planning and resources, but the children aren't responding and they're not learning. I didn't have these problems on earlier placements and am really worried I might fail.*

PRACTICAL TASK PRACTICAL TASK **PRACTICAL TASK** PRACTICAL TASK **PRACTICAL TASK**

If you were Ed, what would you do? Write down as many ideas as you can think of. Figure 10.2 gives some examples.

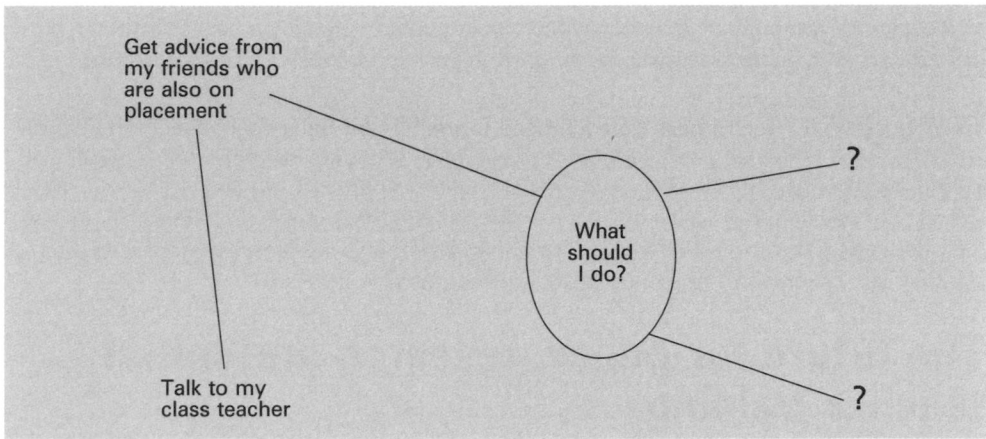

Figure 10.2 Ideas for behaviour management

If you find yourself in a similar situation, consider taking the following steps. Ed's case has been used to illustrate the points. Reflection, as detailed in the previous chapter, is absolutely fundamental to resolving the issues.

- **Reflect on your own preparation and teaching**. In Ed's case, he has reflected on his planning and believes he has done all he can to offer stimulating lessons. However, something is going wrong at the beginning of the lesson. Why aren't the children listening? Is his delivery too slow or too fast? Should he wait until they are all quiet before he starts his introduction?
- **Reflect on your behaviour management strategies**. Should Ed be using different strategies to settle the class? Should he be rewarding those who are listening?
- **Reflect on your relationships with the class.** Ed will need to explore why the children are not responding to him as an authority figure at the start of lessons. Is it related to issues of self-presentation? Has he endeavoured to form relationships with the children?
- **Reflect on the children's relationships with each other.** If several children are responding to peer pressure to not comply with Ed's instructions, there may be a need to strengthen class relationships.
- **Reflect on the children's relationships with curriculum.** Explore the children's relationships with curriculum through talking to them and their teacher – you may gain further insights into their behaviour.
- **What other factors might be impinging on the children's behaviour?** Year 6 is a difficult transition time for children. They can be apprehensive about moving to secondary school and this can be expressed via a lack of interest in the primary school and its curriculum, and in feelings of having outgrown it. Has the school worked with Year 6 and their secondary school partners to ease the transition? Do individuals have difficulties at home or with SEN?
- **Seek advice.** Your reflection can also be undertaken with others. Talk to your friends, teacher, mentor and tutor. Ensure that you make it clear that you have taken reflective and practical steps already. Don't sit and panic: seek help early on in your placement – you don't want to risk failing because you could not find a solution on your own.

Individual children with highly challenging behaviour

On occasions, you may be struggling with one child whose behaviour is highly disruptive. For some children, this behaviour might be a response to new personal circumstances such as a separated parent finding a new partner, an impending divorce, a new baby in the home or bereavement. Such cases will demand a supportive responsive from the school.

If a child's behaviour has been a challenge to the school for some time, it is likely that they will have been referred to professionals from external agencies. You will need to work extremely closely with all staff in helping them to implement the plans laid out on the IEP. In the most extreme cases, when the agencies have been unable to help a child improve their behaviour, they may be excluded from the school. This is a last resort as every attempt possible will be made to retain the child in mainstream education.

The future for policy, research and initial teacher training

Behaviour will always be an issue of concern for all stakeholders in education. As you saw in Chapter 1, these stakeholders include not only yourselves, staff in schools, children, parents/ carers, governors and teacher trainers but also members of society who want to live in safe communities. Thus any government will always need to monitor its policies on behaviour and related social issues such as community cohesion, and will inevitably create new ones, as it has done with ECM.

Research plays an important role in informing policy and research into best practice will continue to be undertaken. Past government inquiries such as the Elton Report (1989) often remain influential, and you will also need to remain informed of current inquiries such as the Steer Reports (2005, 2006, 2008) and the new initiatives which emanate from their recommendations. Further, Ofsted's inspection findings will continue to inform all concerned alongside new research.

As for future trainees, the Training and Development Agency for Schools (TDA) will undoubtedly continue to monitor NQTs' evaluations of their preparation for behaviour management during their initial teacher training. Where there are concerns about irregular provision among providers, action will need to be taken to explore best practice so that institutions can improve their courses. At the same time, institutions will gather their students' opinions through module evaluations and amend their teaching in response to comments. You could help your tutors by feeding back on how well prepared you feel to manage children's behaviour.

REFLECTIVE TASK

Prior to teaching on placement, how confident do you feel about behaviour issues? Remember, it is normal to have some anxiety. Which experiences in university and/or in the classroom have taught you the most about children's behaviour? What would enhance your learning, and that of future trainees, in this area?

Your future

Schools cannot solve all behaviour problems by themselves and cannot be expected to – and this is comforting for you, as you cannot be expected to solve all of the more challenging behavioural problems in your class by yourself. You will, however, need to be able to demonstrate that you recognise all of the components involved in preventing (and managing) behavioural issues and have implemented as many of them as possible, both alone and in collaboration with others. Follow the Behaviour4Learning approach and emphasise positive behaviour.

Behaviour is not an 'add on'; it is integral to learning and to your lesson preparation. Affirming relationships are fundamental to being human and have a significant bearing on our behaviour for learning. As Garner (2005) states, positive relationships do not occur by chance – they need to be built. So, take pleasure in getting to know your class, embrace each child as an individual and enjoy the positive behaviour they will exhibit in their eagerness to learn.

A SUMMARY OF **KEY POINTS**

> **Develop your range of behaviour management strategies which include those provided within the Behaviour4Learning framework.**

> **When reflecting on your behaviour management also consider the relationships aspect as emphasised by Behaviour4Learning.**

> **Remain informed of developments in research and policy in behaviour.**

MOVING *ON* > > > > > > MOVING *ON* > > > > > > MOVING *ON*

Learning to manage and understand children's behaviour will never stop, but try not to feel daunted by that thought. Given that behaviour and learning are inextricably linked, the Core Standards guide you through all relevant aspects. These points are not simply related to 'behaviour management' but also to the intricacies of planning, delivering, assessing, reflecting and working collaboratively. This section summarises the main relevant Core Standards for you.

You will need to establish fair, trusting, supportive and constructive relationships not only with the children (C1) but also with their parents, carers and your colleagues in a collaborative and co-operative way (C4a, C4b, C4c, C41). By promoting children's self-control, independence and co-operation via the development of their social, emotional and behavioural skills (C39), this can help them to build stronger relationships with others. You will develop relationships with the key people and agencies identified in this book (C4, C5). It will be essential that you are fully committed to working in a co-operative and collaborative style (C6) and recognise that you are a team member who should also share the development of effective practice with them (C40).

New research and new policy will add to your increasing experience to continually inform you. Hence you need to ensure that your knowledge of behaviour and teaching and learning strategies is up to date and that you can adapt and personalise them as appropriate to your pupils (C10, C15). You will provide a clear positive framework for discipline which is in accordance with the school's policy (C38a). Where children's behaviour is a concern and there is need for outside agencies, you should be able to determine when you need to draw on the expertise of colleagues (C21). To do so will require an understanding of the current legal requirements and national policies on the promotion of children's well-being (C22), as well as an understanding of the roles of colleagues such as the SENCO (C20). Alongside these more practical tasks, you will need to develop the children's relationships with self and others throughout the curriculum (C16).

In order to enhance your practice you will need to take a reflective approach and improve it through undertaking professional development and acting upon advice and feedback (C7, C8, C9). By undertaking these steps, you will be able to impact more fully on children's learning, attainment and well-being (C35) – which will be evident in their positive behaviour for learning.

FURTHER READING FURTHER READING FURTHER READING FURTHER READING

Behaviour4Learning website, www.Behaviour4Learning.ac.uk In addition to covering the theoretical components of the B4L approach, the website will keep you up to date with current developments in research, policy and practice. Revisit it regularly.

Garner, P (2005) Behaviour for learning: a positive approach to managing classroom behaviour, in S Capel, M Leask and T Turner (eds) *Learning to teach in the secondary school: a companion to school experience.* Abingdon: Routledge. Although Garner's book chapter is aimed at secondary schools, it describes the principles of B4L very clearly, raising pertinent issues.

The Teachernet website is a valuable resource for current updates on policy and practice on all areas related to the profession, including children's behaviour. It is available from www.teachernet.gov.uk

The Training and Development Agency for Schools (TDA) has the *Professional Standards for Teachers* available on its website. You will need to be fully aware of the Standards for QTS and for your induction year. You can download them at: www.tda.gov.uk

REFERENCES REFERENCES REFERENCES REFERENCES REFERENCES REFERENCES

Elton Report (1989) *Discipline in schools. Report of the committee of inquiry.* London: HMSO

EPPI (2004) *A systematic review of how theories explain learning behaviour in school contexts.* Available at www.behaviour4learning.ac.uk

Garner, P (2005) Behaviour for learning: a positive approach to managing classroom behaviour, in S Capel, M Leask and T Turner (eds) *Learning to teach in the secondary school: a companion to school experience.* Abingdon: Routledge

Steer, A (chair) (2006) *Learning behaviour, principles and practice – what works in schools.* Available from www.teachernet.gov.uk/publications, accessed 4 August 2008

Steer, A (chair) (2008) *Behaviour review, paper 3.* Available from www.teachernet.gov.uk/docbank/index.cfm?id=12743, accessed 10 September 2008

Steer Report (2005) *Learning behaviour: the report of the practitioners' group on school behaviour and discipline.* London: DfES